Slaying Giants

FINDING YOUR COURAGE AND CONQUERING FEAR

DARLENE SCHACHT

NEW-YORK TIMES BEST-SELLING AUTHOR

Tme-Warp Wife Ministries

TIME-WARP WIFE

Slaying Giants: Finding Your Courage and Conquering Fear

Publisher:
Time-Warp Wife Ministries
114 Wyndham Estate Drive
Steinbach, Manitoba
R5G 2H6

Interior design by Darlene Schacht
Cover design by Darlene Schacht

Interior images provided by Bigstock.com
Cover image by Bigstock.com

ISBN 978-1-988984-16-2

If you wake up feeling fragile, remember that God is not,
and then trust him to be everything you need today.

– John Piper

Table of Contents

About the Author

DARLENE SCHACHT is an award-winning and *NY Times* best-selling author. She is the founder of Time-Warp Wife Ministries, an online publication that encourages women to live Christ-centered lives. Her passion for scripture and hunger for truth is the driving force behind a unique ministry that offers Bible studies and daily marriage prayers.

She began her publishing journey in 2011 working alongside actress/author Candace Cameron Bure to publish *Reshaping it All: Motivation for Spiritual and Physical Fitness.*
With a passion for Jesus, Darlene continues to write, sharing the gospel with countless women around the world.

Visit Darlene's blog at TimeWarpWife.com to find Bible studies, devotionals, and daily marriage prayers.

Other Studies by Darlene Schacht

A Journey
Through
Exodus
Bible-Study Journal
Darlene Schacht,
The Time-Warp Wife

DARLENE SCHACHT
NEW YORK TIMES BEST-SELLING AUTHOR
PURSUING CHRIST
THROUGH THE
LIFE-CHANGING STORY
of Ruth
AN ILLUSTRATED
BIBLE STUDY

the full
ARMOR
OF GOD
BIBLE STUDY
Darlene Schacht
The Time-Warp Wife

Hebrews
BIBLE STUDY
Jesus Christ
King, Redeemer,
High Priest
Darlene Schacht,
The Time-Warp Wife

Philippians
THE JOY OF CHRISTIAN LIVING
4-WEEK BIBLE-STUDY JOURNAL
DARLENE SCHACHT, THE TIME-WARP WIFE

THE BOOK OF
Romans
BIBLE-STUDY JOURNAL
Darlene Schacht,
The Time-Warp Wife

PAUL'S LETTER TO THE
Galatians
BIBLE-STUDY JOURNAL
DARLENE SCHACHT, THE TIME-WARP WIFE
WITH WENDY SADDLER

Faith &
Provision
4-WEEK BIBLE STUDY
JOURNAL
DARLENE SCHACHT, THE TIME-WARP WIFE

Trust in the Lord with all your heart and
lean not on your own understanding;
in all your ways submit to him, and
he will make your paths straight.

Proverbs 3:5-6

Chapter One

LEARNING TO LEAN

Read: 1 Samuel 17 & Numbers 13

Two years ago, I had myself an anxiety attack. A full out knee-knocking, heart-pounding, mind-racing day when all I wanted to do was crawl back into bed and stay there, for a decade or two. I'd never experienced fear like this before–at least not physically. But there I was pacing the floor, gasping for air, and desperately needing a hug.

Shortly after, Michael came home, and as per usual he brought light to my life. You see, my husband has a way of comforting me. He's like a tub of Rocky Road ice cream at the end of a horrible day. He's thick-skinned and wise, taking difficulties in stride while I am more of a mull-it-over-until-I'm-terrified kind of girl–or at least I was that day.

We prayed together, and while I decided to leave it all in God's hands, I didn't quite follow through. Day two was bad, and day three even worse… I was facing a giant and I wasn't prepared.

You see, confrontation is my Achille's heel. You can throw pretty much anything at me, and I'm rock solid, but tell me that someone is angry with me, and I fold like a dollar-store lawn chair.

It's not good. Trust me, I know. The Bible is clear when it comes to the topic of fear and trusting God in all situations, yet somehow spiders, heights, snakes, roller coasters, and angry people find a way to wiggle their way in and disrupt our otherwise peaceful lives.

WE ALL EXPERIENCE FEAR

Looking to the Bible, we find several people who experienced fear in one way or another:

- Elijah was afraid of the soldiers sent by Jezebel
- David was afraid when Saul was seeking to kill him
- Jeremiah was afraid of the king of Babylon
- Moses was afraid when he killed the Egyptian
- Abraham was afraid when he went to Egypt with Sarah
- Jacob was afraid that Esau would kill him
- Gideon was afraid of his family and the men of the town
- Hezekiah was afraid of the armies of Assyria
- Peter was afraid to be recognized as a follower of Christ
- The disciples were afraid of the storm on the sea
- The disciples were afraid of the Jewish leaders after the crucifixion of Christ

We all experience fear, but we don't have to be ruled by that fear. That's what this book is about. Overcoming our fear and walking in faith.

It starts by digging into the Word to learn from the faithful ones who have gone on before us, while leaning on the wisdom of God.

There are times when His wisdom doesn't make sense to us, like the day Elisha told Naaman to go wash himself in the Jordan River seven times, or how Jesus waited two days before going to see Lazarus, even though he knew of his illness. We might wonder where God is taking us or how our situation could work out for the good. But nevertheless, we practice leaning again and again.

You might remember the old hymn "Learning to Lean," by Jeannie Vee Clattenburg. If you don't know the hymn, look it up on YouTube, and let the words sink in. In the first verse she writes,

Learning to lean
Learning to lean
I'm learning to lean on Jesus
Finding more power than I've ever dreamed
I'm learning to lean on Jesus

The more we lean, the more we grow, and as we grow, we discover the strength of His unfailing power. A power that moves us, leads us, and enables to step out in faith and conquer our fear.

Moses Leaned on the Lord

Back in the day, we didn't have all that much when it came to television. For years, we had three channels on a black and white TV with "rabbit ears" that we had to adjust. By the mid 70s, technology advanced, and with it we saw Charlton Heston raising his rod and parting the sea in full color. In fact, we got to watch it every year around Easter.

Whenever I picture Moses, I also picture him holding a staff. As you read through the Exodus story you see it mentioned again and again, but why? Why was it mentioned so often? And what was the significance, if any, behind it?

The answer is two-fold. The first being that the staff represents the power and the authority of God. He used it to bring forth the plagues, he used it to part the Red Sea, he used it to produce water from a rock, and he used it to strengthen the Israelites in the war against the Amalekites. Moses carried it with him, in the same way that you and I carry the power of God within us.

The second reason the staff was an important part of the story is that it represented his dependence on God. Notice the use of the word staff in Isaiah 36:6, "I know you are depending on Egypt, that splintered reed of a staff, which pierces the hand."

The staff is a symbol of those things we rely on. As Moses carried the staff, he was leaning on God for support in the same way that Jacob leaned on his staff to worship the Lord.

> *By faith Jacob, when he was dying, blessed each of Joseph's sons, and worshiped as he leaned on the top of his staff. (Hebrews 11:21)*

Charles Spurgeon once said,

> "The Puritans were accustomed to explain faith by the word "recumbency." It meant leaning upon a thing. Lean with all your weight upon Christ. It would be a better illustration still if I said, fall at full length, and lie on the Rock of Ages. Cast yourself upon Jesus; rest in Him; commit yourself to Him. That done, you have exercised saving faith."

TRANSFORMING POWER

Ephesians 4:23 talks about being renewed in the "spirit" of our mind. It's not the intellectual part of our mind that's transformed, it's the way that we view the world. It's a mindset where every decision we make flows through that funnel of faith.

The spirit of our mind is strengthened over time as we rely on God and walk in His will. It's being able to say, "Whether this turns out the way that I hope it will, or it all goes terribly wrong, I'm okay because I know that God's in control."

Now, before you think it's all about us and the work that we do, let's look at the words of Paul here,

> *Not by works of righteousness which we have done, but according to his mercy he saved us, by the washing of regeneration, and renewing of the Holy Ghost. (Titus 3:5,)*

An example of this transforming power is clearly seen in the life of Peter as God took him from a place of fear to one of courageous faith. On the night Jesus was betrayed, we read that Peter followed at a distance. And, when a servant girl asked if he knew Jesus, Peter denied Him three times. By Acts Chapter 2, we see that a transformation took place in his life.

In Acts 4:29, the disciples prayed, "Now, Lord, consider their threats and enable your servants to speak your word with great boldness."

> "Transformation is a profound, blood-bought, Spirit-wrought change from the inside out". (John Piper)

This feeling of peace and heightened level of courage doesn't happen because we're powerful, daring, or strong. It comes from our reliance on Jesus, and the Holy Spirit at work in our lives.

PAUSE FOR A MOMENT AND SAY THESE WORDS OUT LOUD:

"GREATER IS HE THAT IS IN ME THAN HE THAT IS IN THE WORLD."

OBSERVING THE PROPHETS

We're told that faith comes by hearing and hearing by the word of God. And so, it's important to study the Word. Not that we would have hope in the prophets we read about, but that we would have hope in the God that they serve, by observing and learning from them.

As we observe the prophets, we see that the faithfulness of God held and protected them. We see that throughout scripture God used the flawed and the few so that we might see His mighty hand at work in their lives.

Imagine how David felt before facing the giant. Was he afraid? Was he facing a giant within before he stood face-to-face with Goliath? Afraid or not, he stepped out in faith, conquered the giant, and brought glory to God.

Every one of the stories or struggles that we read about David was a teaching tool in his life designed to strengthen His faith and draw Him closer to God. Any time he went up against Goliath or Saul he courageously chose faith over fear.

DID YOU KNOW

DAVID'S NEPHEW ALSO KILLED A GIANT. (2 SAMUEL 21) IT GOES TO SHOW YOU THAT COURAGE IS CONTAGIOUS!

OUR CHOICES MAY STING

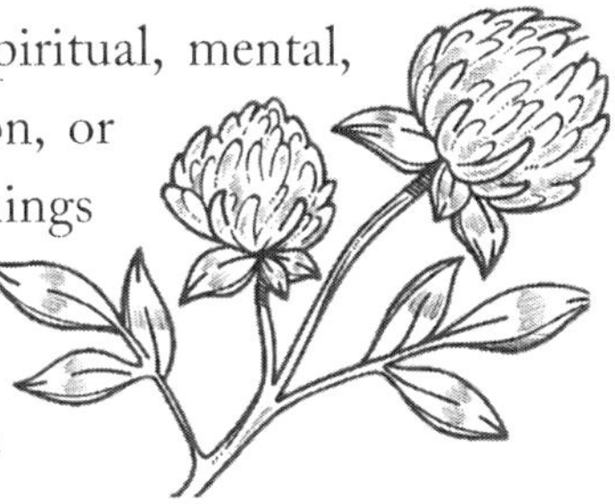

Giants come in many forms. They may be spiritual, mental, physical, or financial. They might be a person, or they may be a problem, but there are two things they all have in common. One is that they threaten our sense of peace, and the other is that they are bread to our soul. We'll talk more about this in the next chapter.

Some days I feel like I'm facing a giant—an insurmountable problem that won't go away. If I face it, I'm taking a risk. If I put myself out there, I might get hurt. If I try, I could fail… And so, I'm left with a choice. I can shrink away from my fear, or I can run toward it trusting that God has a plan.

Courageous faith is willing to say:

- I might get hurt, but I won't be crushed.
- They might not accept it, but I'll try to make peace.
- I might get rejected but I'm choosing love.
- I could get shut down, but I'm going to try.
- This might not be easy, but God's in control.

WE'RE NOT FIGHTING ALONE

Courageous faith tells me that I'm not fighting this battle alone. He goes before me, He's with me, and He'll never leave or forsake me. He goes before us to fight before we even arrive. He softens hearts, opens doors, shuts down the enemy, and gives us faith over fear.

Throughout scripture, God instructs His people to be courageous, and like a shield that stands before a warrior, He stands between us and the enemy.

We've all heard the miraculous story of the parting of the Red Sea. Hemmed into a section of land with the desert on one side and the sea on the other, the Israelites stood firm while 600 chariots raced on in pursuit. As you consider their victory, notice how God positions Himself between Israel and the enemy.

> *Then the LORD said to Moses, "Why are you crying out to me? Tell the Israelites to move on. Raise your staff and stretch out your hand over the sea to divide the water so that the Israelites can go through the sea on dry ground. I will harden the hearts of the Egyptians so that they will go in after them. And I will gain glory through Pharaoh and all his army, through his chariots and his horsemen. The Egyptians will know that I am the LORD when I gain glory through Pharaoh, his chariots and his horsemen."*
>
> *Then the angel of God, who had been traveling in front of Israel's army, withdrew and went behind them. The pillar of cloud also moved from in front and stood behind them, coming between the armies of Egypt and Israel. Throughout the night the cloud brought darkness to the one side and light to the other side; so neither went near the other all night long. (Exodus 14:15-20)*

That thing you're worried about tomorrow, that issue you've been avoiding for a week, that problem you're anxious about today... it's all safe in His hands. In fact, God knew it was all going to happen before you were born.

The Bible tells us,

> *Your eyes saw my unformed body; all the days ordained for me were written in your book before one of them came to be. (Psalm 139:16)*

THESE GIANTS ARE NO MATCH FOR GOD

I have no doubt that the reason behind the story of David and Goliath is to strengthen our faith and bolster our courage. I'm not surprised that David turned down the offer of Saul's armor or that Goliath wore a coat of armor weighing five thousand shekels. Again, it's no surprise that the point on his spear weighed six hundred shekels. And of course, we know that one was a boy and the other a giant. Those details are important because they remind us that the most powerful giants among us are no match against the power of God. Even when that power is funnelled through a young shepherd boy. The faithful, like David and Moses inspire the weakest among us to put fear aside and to lean on the power of God.

DID YOU KNOW

1000 SHEKELS IS EQUAL TO 25.13 POUNDS, WHICH MEANS THAT GOLIATH'S ARMOR WEIGHED ABOUT 125 POUNDS.

Imagine the power you have when God's on your side. The impossible is always possible when He calls you to act. If He's called you to it, He will see you through it.

WALK BY FAITH NOT BY FEELING

Don't let your fear or your weakness keep you from doing God's work. Remember David was just a boy when he killed the giant. Moses was slow of speech when he led the Exodus out of Egypt. Abraham was too old to have children when Isaac was born. Paul was a well-known sinner persecuting Christians beyond measure when God called Him to be an apostle to the Gentiles. God used the weak and the few to show His mercy and power through His saving grace.

Was Jesus afraid? He was afflicted, that much we know. He wept and He was in agony, but knowing the journey ahead, He was still ready and willing to say, "Not my will but Thine be done."

There are some days when I feel more like hiding in my backyard behind a good book than stepping into the spotlight and sharing my faith, because I know there's a good chance I'll get hurt. But wanting and doing are two different things. When we walk by faith we step aside as we invite the power of God to do what we're not able to do on our own.

TRADING GOD'S WISDOM FOR OUR'S

Trading His wisdom for ours can be a little tricky and fearful at times. We're so used to thinking that we're manning the ship, but have you ever noticed how often that ship goes off course?

Stop for a minute to think about this past week. Did every day go as planned? I'm willing to guess that more often than not it didn't. I wake up to changed plans all the time. Just this morning in fact, I got a text that a friend was coming over with her six kids and my daughter was joining us with two more. A house full of children was a welcome departure from the original plan of a quiet day writing outside on the deck.

Yesterday my plans for the day changed again when I got a phone call early in the morning. My daughter asked me to babysit for the day so that they could take the quads out for a ride. Even their plans changed when they found themselves stuck in the middle of a swamp, having to be rescued. It turns out that I didn't get home until 3am.

My point in all of this is that we're not writing the script, God is. He sees today, He sees yesterday, and He sees tomorrow. He sees the heart and the flesh, He sees the struggle, He knows what next year will bring before the sun sets today. Sure, we can make plans, but what happens tomorrow is out of our hands.

THE 12 SPIES

Being courageous doesn't mean that we won't get hurt. In fact, if we're sharing our faith there's a good chance that we'll be facing a giant and we might get some stones thrown our way. Even so, the courageous move forward in faith.

Looking at Numbers Chapter 13, we see that Moses sent out 12 men to explore the land of Canaan. Moses had questions for them: What was the land like? What were the people like? Was the city fortified? Was the soil good? As they planned to invade the land, they needed to know what lay ahead.

After 40 days, the 12 men returned to report what they saw. While the land was flowing with milk and honey, crossing into the land would be met with difficulty. And so, instead of putting their faith in the power of God, ten of them foolishly chose to rely on their strength.

Two of them, on the other hand, looked forward with faith. They believed in the power of God, and knew that with Him on their side, nothing could stand in their way.

DID YOU KNOW

ACCORDING TO JEWISH HISTORY, THE 12 SPIES RETURNED ON THE 9TH OF AV (TISHA B'AV). THIS IS A DARK DAY ON THE JEWISH CALENDAR AS IT'S ALSO THE DAY THAT THE FIRST AND SECOND TEMPLES WERE DESTROYED.

Much like the men in this story, we all have decisions to make when it comes to our future. We have to decide if we're walking in faith or walking in fear. As we continue to go through this study, we'll look at faithful men and women throughout scripture who exercised courage and strength. As we study them, let's remember that these were ordinary people, and that the real hero in all of this was the Lord working in and through them to fulfill His purpose.

PAUSE AND REFLECT

Fill in the spaces:

Moses answered the people, "Do not ____ __________. Stand firm and you will see the deliverance ____ __________ will bring you today. The Egyptians you see today you will never see again. (Exodus 14:13)

The LORD will __________ _____ __________; you need only to ____ __________. (Exodus 14:14)

The Egyptians will know that ___ _____ _______ __________ when I _________ ___________ through Pharaoh, his chariots, and his horsemen. (Exodus 14:18)

What took place between the night Peter denied Jesus and the transformation we see in Acts Chapter 4? (See Acts 4:31)

What does Proverbs 16:9 say? Write the verse out here:

God is always directing your steps. Can you think of any redirection He gave you this past week?

What does Philippians 2:13 say?

Can you think of a particular time when you were afraid to face a situation or person? What or who were you afraid of?

How was the attitude of the ten spies different from that of David? (See Numbers 13:31 & 1 Samuel 17:47)

Look up 1 Samuel 17:45. What weapons did Goliath have, and what was David's defense?

What message did David want to send to those watching the battle? (See verse 47)

What did David do as Goliath moved closer to him? (See verse 48)

Consider the words of Goliath in verse 9. What might this tell us about overcoming our fear? (If you're not sure, you can find a hint in "Week 6, Refiner's Fire")

James 4:13 talks about those who assume they know what tomorrow will bring, but verse 15 shows us a better way of thinking. What is it?

I have told you
these things, so that
in me you may have
peace. In this world
you will have
trouble. But take
heart! I have
overcome the
world.

John 16:33

Chapter Two

FAITH IN HIS POWER

Read: Numbers 14 & Matthew 14

I grew up in the shadow of my sister Bonnie, which is kind of funny, because she's too short to cast much of a shadow. Even so, when it came to personality, she was the star of the show—literally. She played the role of Oliver in our high school musical, and all I got to be was one of many orphaned kids. I guess you could say I was kind of an extra of sorts. I didn't have any lines, I just walked around with a bowl of porridge looking sad with the rest of the cast.

As I got to thinking about that today, I was reminded of Caleb. You don't hear all that much about Caleb. You hear about Moses leading the children of Israel out of Egypt. You hear about Joshua crossing the Jordan and leading the fight in the battle of Jericho, but little attention is given to Caleb, a man of incredible faith. The more I read about him, however, the more I'm intrigued by his courage and spunk.

Caleb's the kind of person you want on your side—loyal, protective, and faithful. In a world of self-centered reliance, his courage was rare. And so, we're going to dig a bit deeper to examine the driving force behind this man of immense courage and strength.

DID YOU KNOW

THE WORD CALEB MEANS "DOG," AND RIGHTLY SO, AS HE FEROCIOUSLY PROTECTED THE CHILDREN OF GOD. HE WAS SPIRITED, LOYAL, AND FAITHFULLY COURAGEOUS.

WE'RE NOT WALKING ALONE

In the last chapter, we talked about the 12 men that Moses sent out to spy on Canaan. In that same chapter we read,

> *When they reached the Valley of Eshkol, they cut off a branch bearing a single cluster of grapes. Two of them carried it on a pole between them, along with some pomegranates and figs. (Numbers 13:23)*

What they were carrying is what's known in the Bible as "firstfruits." The word "first" thus signifying that there is a series to follow. In other words, this was merely a sample of many blessings to come.

In his book, *The Holy Spirit: Activating God's Power in Your Life*, Billy Graham explained this concept of "firstfruits" by saying:

> "One of New York's leading grocery stores exhibited a basket of choice and beautiful grapes in the window. A notice appeared

above the basket announcing: 'A whole carload like this sample basket is expected in a few days.' The grapes were a 'pledge' of what was to come. The firstfruits are but a handful compared with the whole harvest."

Do you see the significance of the grapes and the pole between two of the men? It's symbolic of our Savior, "the firstfruits of those who have fallen asleep." They weren't walking alone on their journey—they were walking with Christ, as they carried the symbolism of the cross, and His blood that was shed.

Remember how God walked with the Israelites in the desert? Remember the fire and the cloud?

Nehemiah 9:19 says,

Because of your great compassion you did not abandon them in the wilderness. By day the pillar of cloud did not fail to guide them on their path, nor the pillar of fire by night to shine on the way they were to take.

BECAUSE GOD IS WITH US WE NEED NOT FEAR WHAT IS AHEAD OF US.

– UNKNOWN

In the same way God was with His people in the wilderness, He was with the twelve men who went to spy out the land, but most of the men failed to see this. Instead of putting their faith in the power of God, they foolishly chose to rely on the power of man.

Out of twelve men, only two of them had the courage to stand up against the enemy and fight for the land that God was giving them. What did they have that the other men didn't? They believed that God would fulfill the promise He made to them.

THEY ARE BREAD FOR US

Notice what Caleb says in Numbers 14:9,

> *Only rebel not ye against the Lord, neither fear ye the people of the land; for they are bread for us: their defence is departed from them, and the Lord is with us: fear them not. (Numbers 14:9, KJV)*

"They are bread for us," he said. You see, Caleb saw what many Christians fail to see—that trials are the very thing that strengthen us. That the giants we conquer are as bread to our soul, and by the power of God working in us and through us, we grow.

We've all found the courage to face obstacles in our lives. Days when we put aside fear to step out in faith. After all, there are some things we just can't avoid. And then, there are people like David and Caleb—even people you may know today—faithful servants who run to the battle, leaving behind the comforts of home to glorify God.

In Joshua Chapter 14, we see Joshua dividing the land up between the families. Because of Caleb's faithfulness, however, the land was promised to him. And so, rather than simply assigning a piece of land to Caleb, Joshua gave him a choice. And what did he choose? To dwell in the land of the giants.

> *"I am still as strong today as I was 45 years ago," he said, "and I'm just as ready to go out to battle now as I was then. Give me the land that the Lord promised me that day and let me go after the giants. With the Lord on my side, I will drive them out just as he said!" (Paraphrased from Joshua 14:10-12)*

How often are we willing to say, "Give me this trial?" How many of us are willing to joyfully take on a giant or run to the battle when it comes our way?

WE CAN MINIMIZE OUR FEAR

If you look at an object in the distance while you're driving, you'll notice that the closer you get to that object, the larger it is. Let's say it's a mountain. It might look like a hill from a distance or merely a bump in the road. In the same way, once you get past that object, you'll notice it decreases in size. There's a simple reason for this. Our field of vision is shaped like a funnel that starts in the center of the eye and spreads out. The closer an object is to your eye the more space it takes up in that field of vision.

DID YOU KNOW

ACCORDING TO A STUDY CONDUCTED BY PSYCHOLOGY GRADUATE, TAYLOR SCHMITZ, AT THE UNIVERSITY OF TORONTO, "GOOD MOODS ENHANCE THE LITERAL SIZE OF THE WINDOW THROUGH WHICH WE SEE THE WORLD,"

Now, let's apply that concept to the way we view fear. The more space we give to our fear, the larger it seems. And so, it's not so much that our problems are big per se, it's the space they're taking up in our thoughts, or our mental field of vision. The less we think about them, i.e., problems we dealt with years ago, the smaller they seem. So, how to we minimize them? We take away their ability to live rent free in our minds.

> *We take captive every thought to make it obedient to Christ. (2 Corinthians 10:5)*

When we take our thoughts captive, we decide what goes and what stays. We trade lies for the truth. We pull out the weeds and plant flowers. We fill our minds with thoughts that nourish and encourage the soul. When we do that, we put God front and center in our field of vision, until He's the only thing we can see.

YOU ARE NOT A VICTIM OF YOUR THOUGHTS. YOU HAVE A VOTE. YOU HAVE A VOICE. YOU CAN EXERCISE THOUGHT PREVENTION. YOU CAN ALSO EXERCISE THOUGHT PERMISSION.

– MAX LUCADO, A LOVE WORTH GIVING

TAKE GOD AT HIS WORD

Some Christians look at scripture as a candy bowl in which they pick and choose their favorite colors to satiate their appetite. They're ready and willing to do the light lifting when it comes to serving the Lord but shrink back when the going gets tough.

In high school, we had an incredible art teacher. She taught me how to mix colors, how to hold my brush, and how to see what I might otherwise miss.

"The first rule of art," she said, "is to draw what you see, not what you *think* you should see." You have to accept that reality and perception are two different things as you let your eyes lead your hand.

You see, the reality of God and our perception of Him might not be the same. The way we perceive God dictates the way we respond to God's will. The question is, what is our perception of God? And what is it based on?

Caleb's courage wasn't based on a loose perception of God, or his own ability to fight, it was based on God's promise that the land would be theirs. Notice his words, in Joshua 14:10 where he says, "*Now then, just as the LORD promised, he has kept me alive for forty-five years...*" He had a promise that God would give them the land, and he held to that promise. It's a child-like faith that takes God at His Word and stands by each promise He's made.

Isaiah 41:10 says,

> *So do not fear, for I am with you; do not be dismayed, for I am your God. I will strengthen you and help you; I will uphold you with my righteous right hand.*

In the same way that they were given a promise that God would help them, strengthen them, and fight for them, we've been given the promise of His Holy Spirit. A power within to guide us, teach us, and strengthen us in the spiritual battles we face.

But you will receive power when the Holy Spirit comes on you; and you will be my witnesses in Jerusalem, and in all Judea and Samaria, and to the ends of the earth. (Acts 1:8)

YOUR VIEW OF GOD – HOW BIG YOU THINK HE IS – WILL DECIDE THE SIZE OF YOUR FAITH.

– TONY EVANS

WHO CAN BE AGAINST US?

In Romans 8:31, Paul asks the church, *"If God is for us, who can be against us?"* Paul is reminding them here, that the power of God is no match for this world.

When Moses led the Israelites out of Egypt, Pharoah tried everything within his power to keep them under his thumb, but nothing could stop God's plan from unfolding. When the disciples started the early church, they were met with great opposition. They were beaten, threatened, stoned, and imprisoned, but nothing could stop the gospel from spreading. When Joseph was sold as a slave to the Midianites by his brothers, and later imprisoned for refusing Potiphar's wife, God was using those trials to forward His plan.

Stop for a minute to examine your life. What's stressing you out? What's bringing you down? What's breaking your heart? If you are feeling down or afraid, don't lean on a loose perception of God or on your own ability to fight—lean on the promises of God. Open your Bible and start highlighting some verses. Remind yourself often that you're not fighting alone. Pray, asking God for peace, and power, and strength. Have faith that He's at work in your life even on the days you can't feel it.

The more we read, the more we see the importance of hardship. We see the value of trials and the potential they have to make a person grow. We read the words, "I will strengthen and help you," and we know that we're not going through this alone.

When we're called according to His purpose, we have the assurance that all things will work out for good.

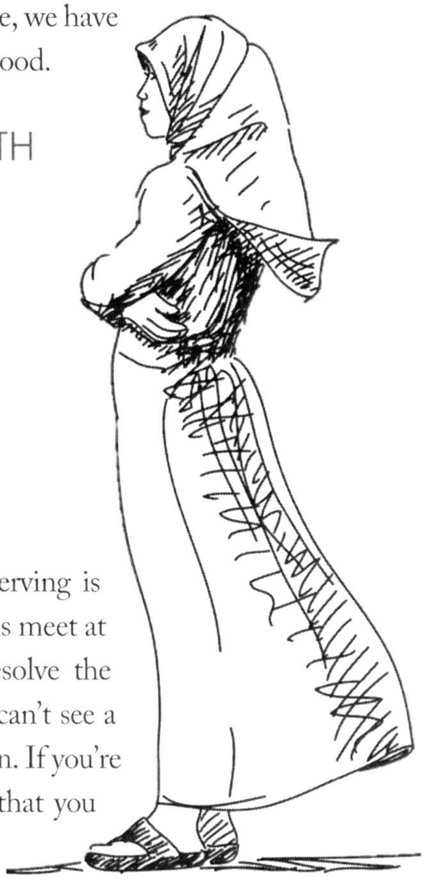

THE SOURCE OF OUR STRENGTH

Some days we say, "I can't do this,"

I'm not good enough
I'm not strong enough
I'm not smart enough
I'm not tough enough
I'm not experienced enough
I'm not brave enough

But here's the thing—the God that you're serving is more than enough. Maybe you can't make ends meet at the end of this month. Maybe you can't resolve the problems in your marriage. And perhaps you can't see a way of this difficult situation you find yourself in. If you're feeling that way, it's time to remind yourself that you serve a God Who specializes in miracles.

On the flip side, some days we take too much credit for things. We forget that there's a driving force behind us. "I did it!" we say. And in that moment of victory, we forget that the power of God is at work in our lives.

I finished my course.
I published a book.
I got the job.
I sold my first piece of art.
I graduated from college.
I found the man of my dreams.
I killed 10,000 men with a donkey's jawbone (this last one is from the story of Samson in case you're wondering!)

Sometimes we need a dry spell—a difficult day to remind us of the source of our strength.

WE MIGHT NOT SEE THE HAND OF GOD

In Matthew Chapter 14, we read how Jesus sent His disciples on ahead of Him in a boat. Later that night, as the wind picked up, they were buffeted by the waves.

Shortly before dawn, Jesus stepped onto the lake and started walking toward them. They didn't recognize Him, and so, at first, they were afraid. As you're reading this story, stop to consider three things:

1. This happened shortly before dawn
2. Jesus walked toward them in the storm
3. They didn't recognize Jesus

Isn't that how life is some days? It's always darkest just before dawn. The storm is raging, the waves are crashing, we're rowing hard against the winds of adversity, and it would seem that our Savior is nowhere to be found, but sometimes we don't recognize Him in the storm.

We might not see the hand of God when we're grieving. We might not feel the warmth of His comforting arms when we're facing our fears. Why? Because perception is deceiving at times. Our brains like to fit God into the comfortable box it's prepared for Him, instead of taking God at His Word.

DID YOU KNOW

IN 1986 AN ANCIENT FISHING BOAT WAS DISCOVERED ON THE SHORE OF THE SEA OF GALILEE. ALTHOUGH THERE'S NO EVIDENCE LINKING "THE JESUS BOAT" TO HIM OR HIS DISCIPLES, IT DOES GIVE US AN EXAMPLE OF THE TYPE OF BOAT THEY MAY HAVE HAD. (WIKIPEDIA)

STEP OUT IN FAITH

Like Caleb, Peter intrigues me. Maybe it's the fact that he's so eager to serve, or perhaps it's because he's so personable. I see a man who loves much, but sometimes his heart runs faster than his head. He reminds me of a new convert so full of love for God, while learning to take their first steps.

There's a great message behind Matthew Chapter 14. As Peter walks on the water, we learn that trusting in God is key to rising above the cares of this world.

In Psalm 69 David equates his suffering to that of being overcome by deep water,

Save me, O God, for the waters have come up to my neck. I sink in the miry depths, where there is no foothold. I have come into the deep waters; the floods engulf me. (Psalm 69:1-2)

Martin Luther once said, "Faith is taking the first step even when you don't see the whole staircase. I can relate to that thought. When I'm driving on the highway at night, I'm always a bit apprehensive. I can't shake the feeling that the road might suddenly drop off or take a sharp turn. And so, there's an element of faith as I rely on the signs directing my path.

When Peter stepped out of the boat, he stepped out in faith. He was walking on water, until something grabbed his attention and drew his mind away from the Lord.

What was it that grabbed Peter's attention? It was the wind.

Wind symbolizes adversity, and, if you know anything about adversity, you know that it can either strengthen or weaken you. Any time we choose faith over fear, peace over stress, or joy over disappointment we're building the resistance muscle that we need to stand strong.

In Matthew Chapter 7, Jesus talks about a foolish man who built his house on the sand saying,

And the rain descended, and the floods came, and the winds blew, and beat upon that house; and it fell: and great was the fall of it. (Matthew 7:27)

As we learn from the story of Peter in Matthew Chapter 14, the key to rising above adversity is two-fold:

1. We need to always keep our eyes on the Lord. Problems, difficulties, worries, concerns... they all have a way of distracting us, and so we need to be careful that we're not so focused on our trouble that we lose our focus on God.
2. We need to reach out to the Lord as our source of strength. Psalm 50:15 says, *Call upon me in the day of trouble: I will deliver thee.*

We don't serve a God Who steps aside when trouble comes. We serve a God Who walks toward us in the storm and sits beside us in the boat. We serve a God Who calms the wind and stills the waves.

The way the world looks at courage is that somehow our minds enable us to face danger. That somehow and someway we're suddenly fearless. A more Biblical way of looking at courage would be a readiness to surrender to God whether we're fearful or not.

Courageous faith says I'll follow the Lord in spite of my fear, the way Caleb and Joshua did as they entered the Promised Land, the way David did when he ran toward Goliath, and the way Peter did when he stepped out of the boat.

The Bible tells us to present our bodies as a living sacrifice, and so we give up ourselves minute-by-minute, day-after-day. We give up our will. We put fear aside. We step out of our comfort zone. We give up control. In return we have a powerful God leading and preparing the way.

PAUSE AND REFLECT

What promise were the Israelites given in Deuteronomy 9:3 as they were about to cross the Jordan River?

What promise do we find in Hebrews 13:5?

Looking at Numbers Chapter 13, list three things that intimidated the spies.

1.

2.

3.

They were especially afraid of the Anakites. Why? (See Deuteronomy 9:2)

Can you think of a trial you've gone through that strengthened your faith? How did you feel at the beginning, were you afraid? How do you feel about it now?

Look up Hebrews 13:6, to finish this sentence. For God has said: Never will I leave you, never will I forsake you. So, we say with confidence:

What does 2 Timothy 1:7 tell us about the Spirit inside us?

What did Joseph say about his struggles in Genesis 50:20? Write the verse out here:

Faith is the bridge between
where I am, and the place
God is taking me.

- Unknown

And who knows but that you
have come to your royal
position for such a time as this?

Esther 4:14

Chapter Three

IF I PERISH, I PERISH

Read: Esther 3-4 & 2 Samuel 10

When Jesus takes the lead, He takes us on a journey through rough terrain and barren land. He leads us to, and through the heart of a storm before He safely leads us out. Why? Because we'll never be complete without the trying of our faith. And so, we're brought down to our knees before we're lifted back up.

We see this throughout scripture as faith is refined through the fire of testing. Joseph is sold into slavery by his brothers. David is relentlessly chased down by Saul. Abraham is asked to sacrifice Isaac. Paul is beaten, tortured, imprisoned, and blind, all for the sake of the gospel.

At the center of each one of their lives, there's one thing that stands out more than anything else. One thing sets them apart from the others. One thing shines bright: which is the simple fact that they lived in obedience to their faith.

YOU'RE HERE TO GLORIFY GOD

If you remember the story of Esther, you might remember this verse from Chapter four:

> *For if you remain silent at this time, relief and deliverance for the Jews will arise from another place, but you and your father's family will perish. And who knows but that you have come to your royal position for such a time as this? (Esther 4:4, KJV)*

These are the words of Mordecai, a father figure to his cousin Esther, both of whom were Jews.

The Bible tells us that he took Esther in and raised her as his own daughter when her parents died. After some time, Esther was taken to the king's palace in Shushan, where she competed in a beauty contest of sorts. The king was in search of a new queen, and so she spent several months in a harem receiving beauty treatments under the care of a eunuch. In the tenth month, she was taken to the king, at which time she won both his favor and the crown.

While Esther was in the palace, a battle ensued between her cousin Mordecai and Haman, one of the highest officials in the palace. The Bible says,

> *Having learned who Mordecai's people were, he [Haman] scorned the idea of killing only Mordecai. Instead, Haman looked for a way to destroy all Mordecai's people, the Jews, throughout the whole kingdom of Xerxes. (Esther 3:6)*

This is why Mordecai was pleading with Esther. She wasn't at the palace for any other reason than to glorify God, and Mordecai knew that. He pointed out her divine purpose by saying, "And who knows but that you have come to your royal position for such a time as this?" In other words, why else would you be there?

We tend to overlook that, when we're caught up in the hoopla of everyday life. We seem to forget that there's a reason we're here. It's not just a feel-good journey through faith. There's a point to all of this, and so we need to be ready to answer His call.

If we don't, help will surely arise from another place, but in the process, we miss out on the blessings that come to those who courageously allow God to use them.

WE OFTEN DON'T REALIZE THAT WHERE GOD PUTS US IS THE VERY PLACE WE NEED TO BE TO RECEIVE WHAT HE WANTS TO GIVE US.

– PRISCILLA SHIRER

Esther had a good reason to be hesitant that day. She knew that anyone who went to see the king without an invitation was putting their life at risk. In fact, according to the ancient historian Josephus, the king had made a law that when he sat upon his throne, none of his people should approach him unless they were called. Men with axes in their hands stood around his throne in order to punish any that approached him without being called. (Jewish Antiquities, Book 11, Chapter 6, 205)

> *All the king's officials and the people of the royal provinces know that for any man or woman who approaches the king in the inner court without being summoned the king has but one law: that they be put to death unless the king extends the gold scepter to them and spares their lives. But thirty days have passed since I was called to go to the king. (Esther 4:11)*

Being the wife of a king wasn't an exemption from the law. Esther was just as vulnerable as anyone else who dared to enter the room, but here's the thing that made her stand out—she chose to suffer affliction with the people of God.

Most of us aren't like Ésther. We're not living in a palace wearing a crown, and we're not facing the annihilation of our people. Even so, every life comes with own set of challenges, and with those challenges come opportunities to glorify God. Who knows, maybe you're in the position you're in, for such a time as this. Maybe you've been hand-picked by God to face that one thing you fear. How will you answer that call?

> "Fear is often our natural response. We don't have to think of all our reasons to be afraid; fear comes unbidden. But being strong and courageous doesn't come naturally. Often, we have to think through different reasons why we ought to overcome our fears with courage. God calls us to take courage because it doesn't just come naturally; we have to fight for it. Confronted with fears on every side and even from within, courage must be seized". – Jon Bloom, DesiringGod.org

We never know how things will turn out. We can guess what we think might take place, but in the end only God knows. And so, when we put fear aside to take that first step, we're walking in faith.

TO MISS A KINGDOM ASSIGNMENT BECAUSE WE'VE BECOME TOO CAUGHT UP IN OUR PERSONAL KINGDOM IS ONE OF THE GREATEST TRAGEDIES WE COULD EVER FACE.

– DR. TONY EVANS

THE FEAR OF REJECTION

If you've ever apologized to a person after a disagreement, you might be familiar with that feeling of apprehension. That worrisome nagging inside you that says, "this might not go well," or "you might be rejected." In some cases, it doesn't go well. People are people, and they'll do what they do, but that should never stop us from doing what's right.

In the same way, you might have a fear of speaking up and sharing your faith. What if they laugh at me? What if they reject me? What if it ruins our friendship?

The fear of rejection is common, and in many cases, it prevents us from moving forward in life. As a result, we don't resolve conflicts, we don't share our faith, we don't speak up for what's right... We think we're afraid of rejection, but what we're really afraid of is pain. That somehow, we'll be psychologically damaged and unable to heal.

We need to change that way of thinking by reminding ourselves that it's okay to feel pain. It's okay to feel sorrow, and in fact is a natural part of growing in the likeness of Christ.

Jesus said,

If the world hates you, keep in mind that it hated me first. (John 15:18)

In 2 Samuel Chapter 10, we're told that after the king of the Ammonites died, David reached out to his son.

"I'll show him some kindness," he said, "in the same way his father showed kindness to me."

And so, David sent his men to the land of the Ammonites to express his sympathy to the king. It didn't go well. Suspicious of David's intentions, the king responded with violence. We read,

Hanun seized David's envoys, shaved off half of each man's beard, cut off their garments at the buttocks, and sent them away. (2 Samuel 10:14)

Humiliated, the messengers returned to David, who told them to stay in Jericho until their beards grew back in. Unfortunately, however, that wasn't the end of it. When the Ammonites realized they insulted David, they pushed all the more, gathering thousands of men for a battle. On hearing this, David sent Joab out with the entire army of fighting men. (v. 7)

WE NEED TO REACH OUT

What started out as an act of kindness, turned into a battle between Israel and Ammonites. Surrounded by armies both in front and behind them, Joab divided the troops into two groups. Putting one group under the command of his brother, Joab instructed him:

> *If the Arameans are too strong for me, then you are to come to my rescue; but if the Ammonites are too strong for you, then I will come to rescue you. (2 Samuel 10:11)*

DID YOU KNOW

FIGHTING BACK-TO-BACK WAS COMMON IN ANCIENT WARFARE, AS IT GAVE THE SOLDIERS AN OPPORTUNITY TO WATCH THE ENEMY FROM ALL SIDES. IT'S ALSO WHERE THE PHRASE, "I'VE GOT YOUR BACK," STEMS FROM.

Joab's strategy illustrates the importance of supporting our brothers and sisters in Christ. It reminds us that:

a) We are not fighting alone
b) We need to be there for each other
c) Sometimes we need to reach out

We're all part of one body. When one part suffers, we all suffer, which is why it's important to have each other's back. To pray for each other. To comfort one another. To spur each other on. Some days we need to pick up the phone and ask somebody to pray. Whether that's your pastor, your husband, your friend, or your family, you need the strength of the body behind you.

> "God urges us not only to pray and commit our burdens to Him, but to seek out others who will help us carry our burdens by their prayers". —Billy Graham

THE LORD WILL DO WHAT IS RIGHT

Joab was not a perfect man. He was a loyal to David, and yet at times he disobeyed the king's orders. Even so, we can learn from him by examining the approach he took before stepping into the battle,

> *Be strong and let us fight bravely for our people and the cities of our God. The LORD will do what is good in his sight. (1 Samuel 10:12)*

As I read those words, *The Lord will do what is good in his sight*, I was reminded of Esther, and how she trusted the Lord to do what was right. Anytime we step out of our comfort zone and into the battlefield we're taking a chance. A chance that we might get rejected, wounded, persecuted, or shot down. We put ourselves out there for the sake of our faith. We stand up to injustice to protect those who can't. We make amends to illustrate the love and forgiveness of God. We do our best, and trust God with the rest.

What Jesus is telling us here is to do the right thing regardless of what it might cost.

A REFLECTION OF CHRIST

Open your Bible to Esther Chapter 3 and look at verse 12. Notice the date there? It's the 13th day of the first month. Why is that significant? Because, according to the Book of Numbers, it is the day before The Passover,

On the fourteenth day of the first month the LORD's Passover is to be held. (Numbers 28:16)

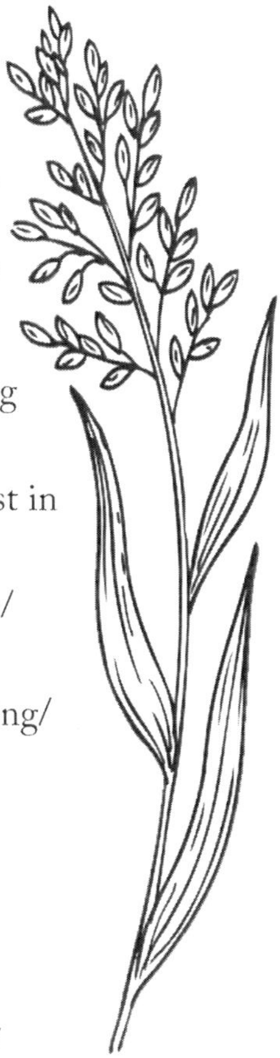

As we look to the New Testament, we see that Jesus was crucified on Passover. And what happened just before He was crucified? We're told that Judas went to the chief priests with a plot to betray Jesus. There's a parallel here between the two timelines as both take place during Passover week.

In addition to that, we see several reflections of Christ in the life of Esther:

- She was willing to lay down her life for her people/ Jesus laid down His life for all mankind
- She was a mediator between her people and the king/ Jesus is a mediator between God and man
- Because of her sacrifice the enemy was defeated/ Jesus defeated Satan when He rose from the dead
- Her people were saved from death/ Jesus brought salvation to the world
- She fasted for three days before going to the king/ Jesus rose from the dead three days after He was crucified

DID YOU KNOW

OUT OF THE 66 BOOKS IN THE BIBLE, ONLY 2 OF THEM ARE NAMED AFTER WOMEN, ESTHER BEING ONE OF THEM.

Like Jesus, who was willing to give up His life, Esther was ready to die for her people, fulfilling the mission for which she was called. Esther teaches us that courage begins by making a choice. A decision to lay down our lives and to pick our cross. A willingness to say, "Yes," to God.

PAUSE AND REFLECT

Fill in the spaces:

> Then Esther sent this reply to Mordecai: "Go, gather together all the Jews who are in Susa, and _________ ________ _______. Do not eat or drink for three days, night or day. I and my attendants will fast as you do. When this is done, I will go to the king, even though it is against the law. And ____ ___ _________ ___ _________." (Esther 4:15-16)

In Luke 9:23 Jesus said, "Whoever wants to be my disciple must deny themselves and take up their cross daily and follow me." What do you think the words "take up your cross" mean?

James 1:2-4 talks about the testing of our faith. What attitude are we to have regarding the trials we face?

According to that same verse in James, what does the testing of our faith produce?

According to 1 Peter 1:7, what do our trials prove?

What does Isaiah 53:3 say about Jesus? Write the verse out here:

What does Jesus say about fear in Matthew 10:28? Write the verse out here:

Courage is not simply one of the
virtues, but the form of every
virtue at the testing point.

– C.S. Lewis

The LORD himself goes before you and will be with you; he will never leave you nor forsake you. Do not be afraid; do not be discouraged.

Deut. 31:8

Chapter Four

HE GOES BEFORE US

Read: Acts 9

Anyone familiar with the New Testament would be familiar with Paul, one of the apostles of the early church. Paul (formerly known as Saul) was instrumental in spreading the gospel to the Gentiles, as well as authoring several New Testament Books. What some aren't as familiar with is how Ananias played a major role in Saul's conversion. We don't know much about Ananias other than a brief mention of him in the book of Acts, but in that one chapter we see the power of courageous faith and how necessary it was in fulfilling his mission.

Turning to the Book of Acts we get a glimpse of who Saul was before his conversion. Chapter 9 verse 1 tell us that he was *breathing out murderous threats against the Lord's disciples.* Earlier on, in Chapter 7, he stood by and watched while an angry mob dragged Stephen out of the city and stoned him for preaching the gospel of Jesus Christ. Chapter 8 clearly states that Saul approved of the violent death that he witnessed. With a mission to destroy the church, Saul went from house to house, dragging both men and women off to prison.

WILLING TO YIELD

Many want to serve God, but the minute it comes with a cost, we see fewer volunteers. No one wants to step onto a mission field that could cost them their life, yet God asked Ananias to put aside his fear, and to submit to His authority when He asked him to go visit Saul.

If we hope to be used for a mission, we must be willing to yield in submission. Ananias was ready to give himself over to God regardless of what that might cost.

> *The Lord told him, "Go to the house of Judas on Straight Street and ask for a man from Tarsus named Saul, for he is praying. In a vision he has seen a man named Ananias come and place his hands on him to restore his sight." (Acts 9:11-12)*

DID YOU KNOW

"STRAIGHT STREET" IS THE ONLY STREET MENTIONED BY NAME IN THE BIBLE. ACCORDING TO WIKIPEDIA, "THE WESTERN HALF OF THE STREET, INCLUDING THE MIDHAT PASHA SOUQ, IS NOW NAMED 'MIDHAT PASHA STREET,' WHILE THE EASTERN HALF, LEADING TO THE BAB SHARQI GATE IS NAMED 'BAB SHARQI STREET.'" (VISIT WIKIPEDIA TO SEE A PHOTO)

Ananias was aware of the danger. The Bible tells us that he had heard the reports, he knew what Paul had done to the believers in Jerusalem, and he knew that Saul was in Damascus for the sole purpose of persecuting followers of Christ. Regardless of how he felt and what fear he might have struggled with, Ananias obeyed God and went to see Saul.

> *Placing his hands on Saul, he said, "Brother Saul, the Lord—Jesus, who appeared to you on the road as you were coming here—has sent me so that you may see again and be filled with the Holy Spirit." (Acts 9:17)*

HE GOES BEFORE US

What Ananias didn't know is the same thing that many of us forget when it comes to the challenges we face—that God goes before us to fight the battle, to soften hearts, and pave the way.

Before Joshua led the people of Israel into the Promised land, Moses encouraged him saying,

> *"The LORD himself goes before you and will be with you; he will never leave you nor forsake you. Do not be afraid; do not be discouraged." (Deuteronomy 31:8)*

In Chapter 1 we talked about the twelve spies that Moses sent to explore the land of Canaan, and how ten of them were afraid to return because of what they had seen.
Moses encouraged them saying,

"Do not be terrified; do not be afraid of them. The LORD your God, who is going before you, will fight for you, as he did for you in Egypt, before your very eyes." (Deuteronomy 1:29-30)

This is the same God that went before them through the desert. They saw the cloud that let them by day and the pillar of light that led them through the night. They saw the hand of God work in miraculous ways, and still failed to see His power and strength.

I LEARNED THAT COURAGE WAS NOT THE ABSENCE OF FEAR, BUT THE TRIUMPH OVER IT. THE BRAVE MAN IS NOT HE WHO DOES NOT FEEL AFRAID, BUT HE WHO CONQUERS THAT FEAR.

– NELSON MANDELA

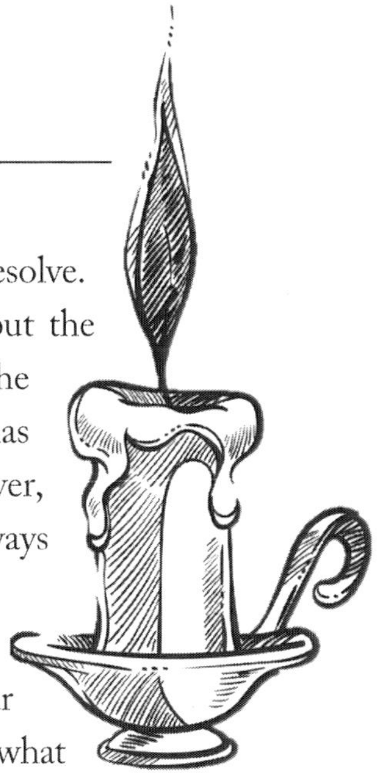

Remember, the problems you face aren't yours to resolve. Yes, we're given a path to walk faithfully through, but the outcome will never depend on our strength alone. In the same way that Esther said, "If I perish, I perish," Ananias knew that following God could cost him his life. However, the rewards that come with following God, will always outweigh the momentary pain that we face.

Every day we make thousands of choices, some of them easy, others not so much. We face giants, we face our fears, and we face trials. Some of them force us to give up what feels good as we choose that which is good. Others move us to step out of our comfort zone to a place of sacrifice as we follow God's will.

People look at courage as though it's the absence of fear, but the fact is that courage is performance in spite of one's fear.

THE DRIVING FORCE BEHIND COURAGE

So, what's the driving force behind courage? Motivation. Let me give you an example. I am terrified of wasps. You won't see me anywhere near a wasp, and if one comes my way, you can bet I'll be running in the opposite direction. On the same note, something happens to me when it comes to the ones that I love. I would hunt down a wasp and kill it before I'd let one bite my grandbabies. Love motivates me to face my greatest fears. It's the same motivation that a father has when he runs into a burning building to save his baby's life, and as believers, we are motivated by a deep love for God.

Elisabeth Elliott is well-known among Evangelical Christians, as one of the bravest souls of our generation. Several years after her husband risked his life, and was killed at the hands of Huaorani warriors, she returned to Ecuador with her young daughter to complete the mission her husband had started. Because of her courageous faith, she was instrumental in leading many of them to the Lord. I think one of the best quotes that sums up her courage is this:

WHEN OBEDIENCE TO GOD CONTRADICTS WHAT I THINK WILL GIVE ME PLEASURE, LET ME ASK MYSELF IF I LOVE HIM.

– ELISABETH ELLIOT

"I think that's a question we all need to ask when it comes to facing our fears. Is our love for God greater than the fear that's holding us back? Imagine a scale where the thing you fear is on one side and your love for God is on the other. Which way is it tipping?

If it's tipping in favor of fear, maybe it's time to ask yourself if your understanding of God might be skewed.

The Bible says,

> *For God hath not given us the spirit of fear; but of power, and of love, and of a sound mind. (2 Timothy 1:7, KJV)*

DID YOU KNOW

THE ORIGINAL WORD USED FOR "POWER" IN 2 TIMOTHY 1:7 WAS "DYNAMIS," WHICH IS WHERE OUR WORD FOR "DYNAMITE" COMES FROM. IT'S MORE THAN SIMPLY POWERFUL, IT'S INCREDIBLY POWERFUL AND EFFECTIVE.

The fear that Paul is talking about is intimidation. It means that we lack assurance in what God can do. That's where it's important once again, that the scale is tipping in God's favor. Ask yourself which is bigger, your problem, or God's ability to solve it.

Courageous faith is a combination of love and trust. It means we both love God, and we trust God. It's a faith that enables us to step out of our comfort zone when the Spirit moves us to do so.

You see, God doesn't need us to accomplish His will, He's fully capable of doing that on His own. What He wants is the opportunity to work through His people. He desires fellowship with us; therefore, He calls us to be His hands and His feet. Not by our strength alone, but by His mighty Spirit that works through us.

It's not our ability He desires, it's our obedience, and so we're often led to places we'd never dream of stepping into. Consider the courageous men and women we read about in the Bible. How they were ready and willing to give up their lives to walk in obedience to God's will. God didn't choose these people because of their strength or their power, He chose them because He desired to use them for His honor and glory.

THE DECEPTION OF COMFORT

We all struggle with courage. There's the one voice that tells us to do what *is right*, and then there's another voice, that tells us to do what *feels right*.

"Take the easy road," it says. "Walk away before you get hurt."

"Don't share your faith, or you might lose a friend."

"If you speak up, you'll look like a fool."

We've heard that voice throughout life. The same voice that tells us to eat that third cupcake. The same voice that tells us to stay in bed when we know that we need to get up. The voice that would rather binge Netflix than go for a walk.

It's almost like we have two brains, one based on fact, and the other on feelings. The Bible describes them by using the terms the "spirit" and "flesh," saying:

For the flesh desires what is contrary to the Spirit, and the Spirit what is contrary to the flesh. They are in conflict with each other, so that you are not to do whatever you want. (Galatians 5:17)

The key to one's courage, is keeping in step with the spirit. For it is through the Spirit and by the Spirit that we are equipped to live victorious lives. It's a challenge, and some days it's a knee-knocking, pulse-racing, experience, but it is the path to the cross that leads us to Christlikeness.

The Spirit leads us in paths of righteousness, but if we hope to follow His lead, we must be willing to surrender our lives to God's will, and to sacrifice anything that stands in the way.

Don't be drawn in by the deception of comfort. Sometimes the greatest blessings in life are just outside the comfort zone. The fear of rejection, the fear of failure, and the fear of pain are just a few of the walls that lock us in and hold us back from moving forward in life.

As I got to thinking about this today, I was reminded of those who gave up the comforts of home to follow the Lord:

But Ruth replied, "Don't urge me to leave you or to turn back from you. Where you go I will go, and where you stay I will stay. Your people will be my people and your God my God." (Ruth 1:16)

By faith Abraham, when called to go to a place he would later receive as his inheritance, obeyed, and went, even though he did not know where he was going. (Hebrews 11:8)

[Moses] chose to be mistreated along with the people of God rather than to enjoy the fleeting pleasures of sin. He regarded disgrace for the sake of Christ as of greater value than the treasures of Egypt because he was looking ahead to his reward. (Hebrews 11:25-26)

Although it is completely irrational at times, we follow our emotions instead of following faith. And what do we miss in the process? The opportunity to be blessed in ways we might never imagine. And so, it's important to get past that wall, or at least be willing to when we know that we should.

MAN CANNOT DISCOVER NEW OCEANS UNLESS HE HAS THE COURAGE TO LOSE SIGHT OF THE SHORE.

– LORD CHESTERFIELD

The Christian life is one of transformation—a readiness to leave sin behind, with an onward motion to the goal ahead. And, as long as we're in the flesh, we are fighting an ongoing battle.

We take our cue from Christ Who knelt to pray on the night He was betrayed, saying, "Not my will but thine be done."

We don't slip into holiness like a comfy recliner. It's more like climbing a mountain through rocky terrain. And by the fruit of the almighty Spirit of God working in us and through us we fight the good fight. We press on to the goal. We crucify the flesh. We cast aside anything that weighs us down. We bring our bodies into subjection. We count all things as loss for the excellency of the knowledge of Christ.

PAUSE AND REFLECT

Fill in the spaces:

The LORD is my light and my

____________________ whom shall I fear? The LORD is the

________________________ of my life—of whom shall I be

afraid? (Psalm 27:1)

In what ways was Paul persecuting the Christians? (See Acts Chapter 9 & 8:3)

What was the driving force behind Ananias courage?

What does the word submission mean according to Dictionary.com?

What are some of the walls that lock us in and hold us back from moving forward in life?

In this chapter, we looked at five people who left their comfort zone to follow the Lord. Who were they?

Courageous faith is a combination of two things, what are they?

Before Joshua led the Israelites into The Promised Land, Moses encouraged him by telling him three things about God. What were they?

1.

2.

3.

Surely God is
my salvation;
I will trust
and not be
afraid.
The LORD,
the LORD
himself, is my
strength and
my defense;
He has become
my salvation.

Isaiah 12:2

For we are God's handiwork,
created in Christ Jesus to do good
works, which God prepared
in advance for us to do.

Ephesians 2:10

Chapter Five

THE BEAUTY OF CRACKED VESSELS

Read: Judges 6 & 7

Looking at the story of Gideon, it's worth noting that he was threshing wheat in a winepress. The Bible tells us that he was there to keep it from the Midianites. Normally the grain was beaten or threshed on a threshing floor where there was ample exposure to the wind. The process that followed, known as winnowing, was used to separate the wheat from the chaff as the winds blew through. Using his pitchfork, a farmer would toss the wheat into the air, and while the seed fell to the ground, the chaff (casing around the seed) was carried away in the wind. Hosea 13:3 compares the wicked to chaff that swirl from the threshing floor.

If you look at an image of an ancient winepress, you'll see a square or circular pit sunk into the ground. It's not a great location for the wind to blow through, and so, this location was highly unusual, but also significant. It wasn't ideal for threshing wheat, but for Gideon, it was a good place to hide out from the Midianites.

TRIBULATION LEADS US TO REPENTANCE

The Midianites were descendants of Midian, a son of Abraham and his second wife Keturah. At this time in history, they were many in number, oppressive, and powerful. Because of the oppression, the Israelites were hiding out for the most part. In fact, the Bible tells us in Judges Chapter 6 that they prepared shelters for themselves in mountain clefts, caves, and strongholds.

With a large number of camels, they were able to swoop in on enemy territory to ravish it quickly, and so they did as they oppressed the Israelites time and again.

Notice what it says in this verse,

> *The Israelites did evil in the eyes of the Lord, and for seven years he gave them into the hands of the Midianites. (Judges 6:1)*

In the same way that God allows us to be tested and tried, this time of tribulation was God's way of waking them up and leading them back to repentance. Now it was time for God's people to fight back, which is where Gideon's mission begins.

GOD SEES OUR POTENTIAL

Looking at verse 12, I can't help but smile as I look at the title God uses to address him.

"The LORD is with you, mighty warrior."

This man was hiding out from the enemy, and God saw him as a mighty warrior. Quite different from the world's view of mighty, but then again God does not look at us through that lens.

Just as He saw the potential in Gideon, God sees the potential in both you and me. He knows we are capable of more than we could ever imagine.

"My clan is the weakest," Gideon said, "and I am the least in my family."

Here is the thing we so often miss. Our accomplishments are not based on who we think we are, they're based on the power of God working in us and through us. When we truly believe in His power and might, we find the courage to stand when we're not so courageous.

IT IS NOT MY ABILITY, BUT MY RESPONSE TO GOD'S ABILITY, THAT COUNTS.

– CORRIE TEN BOOM

DON'T LET FEAR STAND IN THE WAY

Maybe we're not threshing wheat in a winepress like Gideon, but we've all had those days when we're hiding out from the world. Perhaps you can't find the courage to stand up for injustice. Maybe you're struggling to defend your faith and share it with others. Perhaps you've been putting off the one dreadful thing that you know you should do... In any case, today's a good day to put aside fear, step out in faith, and trust God.

"Maybe it will turn out well, and maybe it won't." That's what my sister used to say. She also said, "In any case, you can be sure that God's in control."

The Bible says,

> *Sow your seed in the morning, and at evening let your hands not be idle, for you do not know which will succeed, whether this or that, or whether both will do equally well. (Ecclesiastes 11:6)*

In other words, do your part, and keep doing your part. Don't let your fear stand in the way of what needs to be done. Whether you fail or succeed is up to the Lord. The question is, have you walked in obedience to God's will? Have you done the right thing?

ETERNAL GLORY OUTWEIGHS THE PRICE

Sometimes doing the right thing is the hardest thing you'll ever do, and sometimes it comes with a price. Even so, it could never compare to the glory that God has prepared.

> *For our light and momentary troubles are achieving for us an eternal glory that far outweighs them all. So we fix our eyes not on what is seen, but on what is unseen, since what is seen is temporary, but what is unseen is eternal. (2 Corinthians 4:17–18)*

As we read the story of Gideon, we see that God takes him from a place of self-reliance to a place of complete reliance on Him. We would be foolish to think that there's strength in numbers when it comes to the power of God. It didn't matter that Gideon's clan was the weakest, or that he was the least in his family; God didn't want a mighty army to receive the glory, He wanted to rescue His people Himself. And so, in Judges Chapter 7, we see God pare down Gideon's army of 32,000 to 10,000 men and then again, to a mere 300 before sending them off to the battle. Notice, that's less than 1% of the original size of the army.

> *The LORD said to Gideon, You have too many men. I cannot deliver Midian into their hands, or Israel would boast against me, 'My own strength has saved me.' (Judges 7:2)*

GOD SCORNS AND MOCKS THE DEVIL, IN SETTING UNDER HIS VERY NOSE A POOR, WEAK, HUMAN CREATURE, MERE DUST AND ASHES, YET ENDOWED WITH THE FIRSTFRUITS OF THE SPIRIT, AGAINST WHOM THE DEVIL CAN DO NOTHING.

– MARTIN LUTHER

HE CHOOSES TO USE US

As a parent, it was easier and quicker to do things myself. Even so, I encouraged my children to work alongside me. To wash the dishes, to tidy their rooms, and to help prepare dinner. I knew that learning and working was an important part of the nurturing process, but it was also a way to cultivate our relationship.

In a similar way, we see God working alongside His people. He doesn't "need" us He "chooses" to use us. He longs to be with His children, and so He invites us to be a part of His unfolding story.

God didn't "need" Gideon to fight on His behalf, He wanted him to. And when Gideon was afraid, He encouraged and strengthened Him the way that a Good Father does.

DID YOU KNOW

AFTER GIDEON BROKE DOWN THE ALTAR OF BAAL, HE WAS GIVEN THE NICKNAME "JERUB-BAAL," WHICH MEANS BAAL WILL CONTEND WITH HIM.

Think about the things that you are facing today or this week. Maybe something is worrying you or keeping you up at night. You might wonder how you'll get through it or where you'll find the strength to do what needs to be done. It's important in these situations to remember that we're not the one's solving the problem—we're merely a vessel of His wisdom and power.

Think of it this way: imagine a hammer assigned to the task of building a house. If it had a brain like you and I, the hammer might spend the weekend worrying about how it could possibly work. If only it knew that the driving force behind it would be doing the work, the hammer could rest and relax.

It's silly to imagine ourselves in that state, but some days, that's where we're at. Worrying about things that are out of our hands. Afraid of the things that we can't control... We tend to forget that He can, and more importantly, He does.

Remember, you're not the source of your strength, you are merely a tool in the hands of the Master Builder. And so, the Lord warmly reminds us,

Therefore, do not worry about tomorrow, for tomorrow will worry about itself. Each day has enough trouble of its own. (Matt. 6:34)

Some days even the little things add up to a lot. A lot of worry, a lot of concern, a lot of fear and anxiety... but mostly it's a lot of us needing to let go and let God. Needing to trust Him more than we do. Needing to stand back and let Him do His work. If we're stressed, worried, and overthinking our lives, we're still holding on to the reigns, and we need to let go.

Elisabeth Elliot writes,

We are meddling with God's business when we let all manner of imaginings loose, predicting disaster, contemplating possibilities instead of following, one day at a time, God's plain simple pathway. When we try to meet difficulties prematurely, we have neither the light nor the strength for them yet.

CRACKED VESSELS

Before we close this chapter on Gideon, I want to point out something out to you, which is, both the beauty and the importance of cracked vessels.

In 2 Corinthians 4:7 we read, "But we have this treasure in jars of clay." And why do we have this treasure? Paul finishes the thought by saying, "to show that this all-surpassing power is from God and not from us." What he's talking about here is the message of Christ. When the jar is broken the light can shine through.

Trials, tribulation, pain, and persecution all have a way of pulling back the curtain to reveal what's going on inside. Brokenness gives us the opportunity to lean on God and to show the world the source of our strength. The more broken we are, the brighter we shine!

DON'T SHINE SO OTHERS CAN SEE YOU.
SHINE SO THAT THROUGH YOU,
OTHERS CAN SEE HIM.
– C.S. LEWIS

Charles Spurgeon compares the battle in Judges Chapter 7 to that of a Christian life saying,

> "Gideon ordered his men to do two things: covering up a torch in an earthen pitcher, he bade them, at an appointed signal, break the pitcher and let the light shine, and then sound with the trumpet, crying, "The sword of the Lord, and of Gideon!" This is precisely what all Christians must do. First, you must shine; break the pitcher which conceals your light; throw aside the bushel which has been hiding your candle, and shine. Let your light shine before men; let your good works be such, that when men look upon you, they shall know that you have been with Jesus. Then there must be the sound, the blowing of the trumpet. … Take the gospel to them; carry it to their door; put it in their way; do not suffer them to escape it; blow the trumpet right against their ears."

PAUSE AND REFLECT

Gideon said, "My clan is the weakest, and I am the least in my family." What did Moses say about himself in Exodus 4:10?

Do you ever find yourself talking like Gideon or Moses? What do you say about yourself that might be limiting you?

Judges 6:1 says that God "gave them into the hands of the Midianites." Why did God do that?

What was the first act of courage that God asked of Gideon?

Where were the Israelites hiding from the Midianites?

In Judges Chapter 7, we see God pare down Gideon's army again and again. Why?

Fill in the spaces:

Therefore, if any man be _____ ___________________, he

is _____ ______________ ______________________: old

things are passed away; behold, all things are become

_____________. (2 Corinthians 5:15-17, KJV)

What might the clay vessels in Judges Chapter 7 symbolize? What might the light symbolize?

Blessed is the one who
perseveres under trial
because, having stood the
test, that person will receive
the crown of life that the
Lord has promised to
those who love him.

James 1:12

Chapter Six

REFINER'S FIRE

Read: Daniel 3 & 6

One of the best verses in scripture (although there are many) that sum up the definition of courage is found in Daniel Chapter 3:

If we are thrown into the blazing furnace, the God we serve is able to deliver us from it, and he will deliver us from Your Majesty's hand. But even if he does not, we want you to know, Your Majesty, that we will not serve your gods or worship the image of gold you have set up. (Daniel 3:17-18)

These were the words of Shadrach, Meshach, and Abednego, friends of Daniel, who courageously risked their lives for the sake of their faith.

After the conquest of Judah by King Nebuchadnezzar certain young men from among the Israelites were chosen to serve in the king's palace. Among those men were Daniel, Hananiah, Mishael, and Azariah. Each were giving new names as they were brought into the service of the Babylonian court, as such, Hananiah, Mishael, and Azariah became Shadrach, Meshach, and Abednego.

After some time, they were promoted as administrators over the province of Babylon, but with that promotion came a time of testing. Since idol worship was a vital part of Babylonian culture, King Nebuchadnezzar naturally expected everyone including these men to worship the golden image he had constructed and placed in the province of Babylon. Anyone refusing to worship the statue would be facing immediate execution.

DID YOU KNOW

SINCE RESIDENTIAL TYPE FURNACES WEREN'T REALLY A THING AT THIS TIME IN HISTORY, IT'S LIKELY THAT THIS FURNACE WE READ ABOUT WAS KNOWN AS A SMELTER. SMELTING IS A WAY OF PURIFYING AND EXTRACTING METAL BY THE PROCESS OF APPLYING HEAT.

REFINED BY THE FIRE

Despite the cruel and torturous persecution, they faced, Shadrach, Meshach, and Abednego, courageously stood up for their faith and remained faithful to God. As such, they were sentenced to death by fire. The Bible tells us that Nebuchadnezzar was so angry with them that he ordered the furnace to be heated seven times hotter than it would normally be.

Notice the significance here as the Bible often compares spiritual refinement with the refining of precious metal by fire.

These have come so that the proven genuineness of your faith—of greater worth than gold, which perishes even though refined by fire—may result in praise, glory and honor when Jesus Christ is revealed. (1 Peter 1:7)

Looking to the previous verse, we see that Peter is talking about the grief we experience through the suffering of trials. Like the three men in this story, we're going to have good days. Maybe it's a promotion at work, maybe it's a growing family, or maybe it's just a day when everything is going your way… But, like them, we are going to need courage when we're tested and tried.

Again, Peter writes,

Dear friends, do not be surprised at the fiery ordeal that has come on you to test you, as though something strange were happening to you. But rejoice inasmuch as you participate in the sufferings of Christ, so that you may be overjoyed when his glory is revealed. (1 Peter 4:12&13)

When talking about the refining process, Pastor Jon Courson once said, "The metal worker would know that he was successful in taking out all the impurities when he could look down into that liquid gold and see the reflection of his own face. That's when he knew that the gold was purified."

In other words, the purification process transforms us into the likeness of Christ, the One who chose the way of the cross.

As we look at Verse 25 where we see Nebuchadnezzar looking into the furnace, let's discuss two things that he saw.

First, he saw *four* men in the fire, not three. So, who was the fourth? Nebuchadnezzar described the form of the fourth man as "like the Son of God". It wasn't the son of some god, I firmly believe that it was Jesus, The Son of God.

IMMANUEL, GOD IS WITH US

When the angel appeared to Mary in Matthew 1:23, he said that her son would be named Immanuel. It's a wonderful name because it means that God is with us. We're never alone. Jesus was with the three men in the fire in the same way that He's with you and I when we're walking through the fiery trials of life.

We all have mountain-top days, but I I've come to find that the more time I spend in the valley, the more I'm reminded just how close He is. For it's in those dark times of weakness that I learn to rely on His wisdom and strength.

Think of it this way, what if that one thing you fear turns out to be a pivotal point in your life? What if it's designed to draw you closer to God?

Remember the thief on the cross? His weakest moment was the very thing that led him to Christ. That tells us a lot about the power of weakness, doesn't it?

But look at what Jesus said,

> *And Jesus said unto him, Verily I say unto thee, Today shalt thou be with me in paradise. Luke 23:43, KJV*

You know what I love most about that verse? Those two little words, "with me." We are not in the fire alone. God was with David when he was running from Saul. He was with Moses when he crossed the Red Sea. He was with Joseph in prison. He was with Esther in The

Palace of Shushan. He was with these three men in the fire, and He's with you and me.

David said,

> *Even though I walk through the darkest valley, I will fear no evil, for you are with me; your rod and your staff, they comfort me. (Psalm 23:4)*

When I was a little girl, afraid to sleep in the dark, I found comfort in the simple reminder that I wasn't alone. In fact, I used to visualize Jesus and His angels standing beside me some days. Some nights, I would even point them out to my mom before closing my eyes.

Even now, I still need reminding at times. Whether I'm dealing with poverty, loss, sickness, persecution, or pain—I know that I am never alone. Yes, I might have to go through the fire, but I won't be alone in that fire, I know that for sure.

RELEASED FROM OUR FEAR

Now, let's look at the second thing the king noticed: they were unbound and unharmed. The Bible specifically tells us that they were firmly tied up when they went in, in fact it is mentioned three times in Daniel Chapter 3. I think the reason its stated so clearly is because this part of the story is significant.

It teaches us that although affliction is tough, it can also be freeing, as we are loosed from the things that once bound us. When we stand firm in faith we overcome the enemy, we rise above tribulation, and we conquer our fear.

I touched on this in Chapter 1. I asked you to consider the words of Goliath in 1 Samuel 17:9,

> "If he is able to fight and kill me," he said, "we will become your subjects. But if I overcome him and kill him, you will become our subjects and serve us."

Instead of being enslaved by the enemy, David conquered the enemy which in turn enslaved them.

THE ENEMY DEFINES US BY OUR STRUGGLES, BUT GOD REFINES US THROUGH OUR STRUGGLES.

– JENNIFER ROTHSCHILD

In his letter to the Romans, Paul writes,

> *The Spirit you received does not make you slaves, so that you live in fear again; rather, the Spirit you received brought about your adoption to sonship. And by him we cry, "Abba, Father." (Romans 8:15)*

We have the power to overcome the enemy. That power is a roaring lion within us waiting for the moment we open the door. It is the attunement to God's power and the freedom to release that power that allows us to overcome fear.

Jumping ahead a few chapters, we find a similar story as Daniel was also sentenced to death when he defied the king's order.

It is not a coincidence that these men were selected by God. They were chosen because they were faithful. They were used by Him because they were ready and willing to stand by their faith regardless of what it might cost.

DID YOU KNOW

ACCORDING TO THE LAW OF THE MEDES AND PERSIANS NO DECREE OR EDICT THAT THE KING ISSUED COULD BE CHANGED. (COMPARE DANIEL 6:15 WITH ESTHER 8:8)

When Daniel heard about the decree, he didn't step back from his faith or cower in fear. He went home, and with the windows wide open, he continued to pray three times a day in the same way he had been praying for years. He knew there may be a cost for his actions, but that didn't deter Him from serving the Lord. Daniel had an intimate relationship with God peppered with powerful prayer, laced with obedience, and grounded in faith.

TRIALS ATTEST TO OUR CHARACTER

The faithful aren't always blessed in the way we expect God to bless us. Some days our faithfulness leads us straight to the lion's den where we are further tested and tried. It's in those moments of darkness and fear we need to remember that He rewards those who faithfully seek Him.

> *Blessed is the one who perseveres under trial because, having stood the test, that person will receive the crown of life that the Lord has promised to those who love him. (James 1:12)*

It's easy to say that we trust God, but will we trust Him when we are tested and tried? We can say that we love God, but will we still love Him when things don't go our way? Trials have a way of proving our faith. The Bible says that suffering produces perseverance, and perseverance character. What it's really saying there is that perseverance proves the *validity* of our character.

Daniel Chapter 6 begins by outlining Daniel's goodness and his exceptional character. As we read further on in the chapter, we see how his actions testify to that character.

CHARACTER CANNOT BE DEVELOPED IN EASE AND QUIET. ONLY THROUGH EXPERIENCE OF TRIAL AND SUFFERING CAN THE SOUL BE STRENGTHENED, AMBITION INSPIRED, AND SUCCESS ACHIEVED.

– NICK VUJICIC, UNSTOPPABLE

Throughout scripture we see men like Daniel and his three friends, who chose to put fear aside doing all that they could to hold fast to their faith. Instead of evading their trials, they trusted God enough to walk through them.

And what was the secret to their unwavering faith? Elizabeth Elliot said it best when she wrote, *"The secret is Christ in me, not me in a different set of circumstances."*

Have you ever considered the fact that maybe instead of changing the world around you, God wants to transform the heart within you? Maybe that one thing you fear is designed to keep you grounded and focused on Christ. It's there to show you the life-changing power of faith, and to strengthen the spirit within you.

PAUSE AND REFLECT

What can Daniel 3:17-18 teach us about our attitude during times of testing?

According to 1 Peter 1:7, what do trials prove?

What two things did Nebuchadnezzar see when he peered into the furnace?

Why was the fourth man in the fire significant? What comfort can we personally glean from that?

Why couldn't the administrators and satraps find anything to charge Daniel with?

Fill in the spaces:

Not only so, but we also glory in our

___________________, because we know that suffering

produces _____________________; perseverance,

___________________; and character, ______________.

(Romans 5:3-4)

How does perseverance prove character?

The Bible tells us that the three men in the fire were unbound. What can we learn from this?

By faith the prostitute Rahab, because she welcomed the spies, was not killed with those who were disobedient

Hebrews 11:31

Chapter Seven

THE SCARLET CORD

Read: Joshua 2 & Acts 16:16-38

Reading Joshua chapter 2, I stop short at the word "prostitute." To the world Rahab was nothing more than a harlot, but to the Lord she's highly esteemed. She's precious, and dear—a beloved child of God. Rahab's so loved in fact, that she is mentioned in Hebrews Chapter 11 alongside other men and women of faith, and again in James Chapter 2 as an example of someone whose faith and actions were both working together.

I think of the many names that I too could be called. We all have labels—sin we would rather leave in the past. Satan will always try to magnify our flaws and make us insecure, in hope that by doing so we lose our courage and turn our eyes away from God. Maybe that's who we were, but that is not who we are when we come to the cross.

> *So, from now on we regard no one according to the flesh. Although we once regarded Christ in this way, we do so no longer. Therefore, if anyone is in Christ, the new creation has come: The old has gone, the new is here! (2 Corinthians 5:16-17)*

That's easy to read, but some days it's not so easy for us to accept. Maybe you failed, maybe you fell, maybe you stumbled, maybe you chose to sin when you knew it was wrong… And, like Rahab, perhaps you have a label or two. But remember, you don't trip over something behind you, when you are marching ahead.

Don't minimize the grace you've been given. If you think that your sin is too big for God, think again. There was a cost for that sin. A price that was paid on the cross by the shedding of blood. God wants to use you, not because of your ability, but because of His great love for you.

THE WORLD BEHIND ME, THE CROSS BEFORE ME

There's a hymn we used to sing in church, called "I Have Decided to Follow Jesus," by Sadhu Sundar Singh. You might remember that it was often played at the Billy Graham Crusades. I remember it well because my dad used to sing it around the house all the time with a big smile across his face and both hands up in the air.

"I have decided to follow Jesus," he'd sing, "no turning back, no turning back."

One of the other lines that stands out to me was this, "The world behind me, the cross before me. No turning back, no turning back."

I can't help but be reminded of Rahab. How she

decided to follow God, turned her back on the world as she knew it, and even though she stood alone, she still pressed on.

Let's look at four courageous decisions she made:

1. She disobeyed the king and risked her life to protect the spies sent by Joshua.
2. Being a Gentile, she adopted a new faith.
3. She gave up the comfort of home, and the only culture she knew.
4. She did all this alone.

DID YOU KNOW

HISTORICALLY, IT WAS COMMONPLACE FOR BROTHELS AND INNS TO OPERATE UNDER THE SAME ROOF. AS SUCH, THIS COULD BE THE REASON THE SPIES ENTERED RAHAB'S HOUSE.

HE CAN USE YOU RIGHT WHERE YOU ARE

Notice that God used Rahab right where she was. She had a home and she used it faithfully to follow the Lord. He didn't send her to a mission field in some far-off land. He used what she had, where she was. In the same way, God can use you right where you are. Don't ever think that being a homemaker or going off to a 9-5 job is any less a mission field than that which is overseas. God has called you to the place you are in, and there's potential there to do great things for God.

Don't get me wrong. God calls people every day to mission fields across the globe, but for the ones who stay behind the opportunities to serve are every bit as vital.

In 1 Samuel 30 we read a story about David and 400 of his men who went out to fight the Amalekites, while 200 of them stayed behind. The Bible tells us that David recovered everything the Amalekites had taken from Judah, including his two wives. After returning with the spoils of war, some of the men selfishly assumed they wouldn't be sharing, but David rebuked them saying, "The share of the man who stayed with the supplies is to be the same as that of him who went down to the battle. All will share alike."

Sometimes God says to one, "You're going to go out to battle." To another, He says, "You're going to stay back, and I'll use you right where you are."

It's a reminder to all of us that some of the best soldiers are working behind the scenes.

Whatever your hand finds to do, do it with all your might. (Ecclesiastes 9:10)

As I look at the Bible, I see God using people right where they are. Mordecai sitting at the king's gate day after day. Nehemiah, the king's cupbearer. Jael, a woman who assassinated the commander of the Canaanite army hiding inside her tent, James, and John two fishermen out on the lake.

We don't need much to serve God, we just need to be willing to answer His call. If all that we have are two hands, let's be faithful with the hands that we have. If all we have is a door, let's open it wide. If all that we have is a pocket of change, let's give. When and if He calls us to step out of our comfort zone, we must be willing to get off our "butts" and courageously follow our faith.

Rahab was true to her faith despite her fear. The two spies told her to hang a scarlet cord in her window, and as soon as they left, she did. She didn't question the reasoning behind it, and she didn't delay.

WHEN WE'RE AFRAID, WE HAVE A TENDENCY TO PRAY AND ASK GOD FOR PEACE BEFORE WE'LL STEP OUT AND DO WHAT FRIGHTENS US. BUT MOST OF THE TIME, WE SIMPLY NEED TO MOVE FORWARD.

– SADIE ROBERTSON

THE SCARLET CORD

The scarlet cord is vital to the story, and here's why. If you look at Joshua Chapter 5 (verse 10), you see that Passover week coincides with the 7-day battle of Jericho. If you remember the first Passover in the Book of Exodus, remember that the angel of death killed all the first-born males in Egypt. To protect their homes, the Israelites marked their door frames with the blood of a lamb. This symbolized their faith in the coming Messiah. When the angel of death saw the blood, he "passed over" that home.

The scarlet cord was a symbol of Rahab's faith in the power of God and the coming Messiah. While she may have feared the king to some extent, it was obvious that she feared God more. She had heard stories about the Israelites and how they crossed the Red Sea. She knew their God was the One true God, and while the rest of the city was frozen with fear she stepped out in faith.

Compare these verses from Joshua and Exodus:

Unless, when we enter the land, you have tied this scarlet cord in the window through which you let us down, and unless you have brought your father and mother, your brothers and all your family into your house. If any of them go outside your house into the street, their blood will be on their own heads; we will not be responsible. As for those who are in the house with you, their blood will be on our head if a hand is laid on them. (Joshua 2:18-19)

Take a bunch of hyssop, dip it into the blood in the basin and put some of the blood on the top and on both sides of the doorframe. None of you shall go out of the door of your house until morning. When the LORD goes through the land to strike down the Egyptians, he will see the blood on the top and sides of the doorframe and will pass over that doorway, and he will not permit the destroyer to enter your houses and strike you down. (Exodus 12:22-23)

DID YOU KNOW

THE TWO SPIES IN THIS STORY-REFERRED TO AS "MESSENGERS" IN THE BOOK OF JAMES-SYMBOLIZE THE WORD OF GOD. RAHAB HIDING THE SPIES IS REMINISCENT OF PSALM 119:11, WHERE DAVID WROTE, "I HAVE HIDDEN YOUR WORD IN MY HEART THAT I MIGHT NOT SIN AGAINST YOU."

As a result of Rahab's obedience to her faith, she was not only saved, but she was also taken in by the Israelites as one of their own. The Bible tells us that God is able to do exceedingly abundantly above all that we ask or think, and He did that very thing in life of Rahab. As we look at Matthew Chapter One, we see her listed as an ancestor of both King David, and our Savior, Jesus Christ.

> HE IS NO FOOL WHO GIVES WHAT HE CANNOT KEEP TO GAIN WHAT HE CANNOT LOSE.
> – JIM ELLIOT

Courage starts by saying yes. Choosing to step out in faith regardless of what it might cost. And, with each step we take we find that God is working in us and through us.

FAITH UNDER PRESSURE

In Acts 16 we read a story about Paul and Silas who were met by a female slave (a fortune teller) as they were going to a place of prayer. The Bible tells us that she was shouting at them. Her shouting continued for days, until Paul finally rebuked the Spirit within her.

As a result, they angered her owners who dragged them into the marketplace to face the authorities. After they were severely beaten, Paul and Silas were thrown into prison where they were given an opportunity to not only share their faith, but to testify to that faith. They did so by remaining calm under pressure and worshipping God from their jail cell.

The story goes on to tell us that a violent earthquake suddenly shook the foundation and opened the doors of the prison. Instead of leaving however, Paul and Silas seized the opportunity to share their faith with the guard on duty that night.

When Paul says, *Follow my example, as I follow the example of Christ.* (1 Corinthians 11:1) He's talking about the testimony he shares through living the gospel.

There's a common saying which goes, "You might be the only Bible that people read."

With that in mind, ask yourself, what do they see? What message are you sending out when you are under pressure, stressed out, or in fear? Do they see a God they can lean on by the way that you are leaning on Him?

Think of it this way: imagine a vineyard in season. Rows of vines, laden with fruit, ready to be picked. To fully enjoy the fruit and to share it with others, it needs to be processed. In fact, if you hope to make wine, it needs to be crushed and pressed to extract the juice from the grapes. Before people had wine presses available to them, they applied pressure by stomping the grapes until they were completely crushed, at which time they could separate the juice from the skin and the stems.

We are a lot like that fruit when it comes to the process of living our faith. Our testimony is produced under pressure, so that the more we're hard pressed the more we pour out the message of Christ. It's in the overcoming of trials that they taste of His goodness and power, and, as He pours Himself in, we pour ourselves out.

Paul writes,

We are hard pressed on every side, but not crushed; perplexed, but not in despair; persecuted, but not abandoned; struck down, but not destroyed. We always carry around in our body the death of Jesus, so that the life of Jesus may also be revealed in our body. For we who are alive are always being given over to death for Jesus' sake, so that his life may also be revealed in our mortal body. (2 Corinthians 4:8–11)

How many of us are willing to be stripped down and severely beaten with rods for the sake of our faith? Paul and Silas didn't choose that for themselves; however, they did choose their reaction to it, which speaks volumes about their faith.

We can't dictate the situations we're given, but we can choose the way we receive them. Our attitude toward life is a medium that God uses to draw others to Him.

As children of light, we're reflecting His light, and so, we must give careful attention to the message we share.

SHE LAUGHS WITHOUT FEAR

When the Bible talks about the woman in Proverbs 31, it tells us that she laughs without fear of the future. I see a woman who is confident in the Lord she serves, and His ability to care for her needs. I see a woman who, like Paul, is even keeled through the ups and the downs, knowing that obstacles offer her an opportunity to grow stronger in faith. I see a woman who has placed her future in His capable hands. Hands that are able to mold and to shape her. Hands that are wisely directing her steps.

PAUSE AND REFLECT

What does 1 John 3:1 say? Write the verse out here:

In your own words, tell us what Rahab told the spies before they went to sleep.

What promise did the men make to her?

Why is the scarlet cord vital to this story?

What three things do the verses from Joshua 2 and Exodus 12 have in common?

Why were Paul and Silas in jail?

What were they doing at midnight?

In this chapter, I wrote, "Our testimony is produced under pressure." What do you think that means?

If we can't dictate our situations, what can we do?

Can you think of any situation in your past or present where God has used you to minister right where you were?

Do not be anxious about anything, but in every situation, by prayer and petition, with thanksgiving, present your requests to God.

Philippians 4:6

Chapter Eight

THE POWER OF PRAYER

Read: Genesis 27, 32, & 33

Have you ever felt like you were facing a mountain, you couldn't possibly climb? Overwhelmed with a situation that was out of control? Overcome by troubles that keep coming your way?

Maybe you accepted the fact that you did all that you could. After all, some things are out of our hands. The thing to remember, however, they're not out of God's. We serve a God Who created all things, and, if He created them, He can very well change them, but it must start with prayer. The unwavering, persevering, power of prayer.

> *Do not be anxious about anything, but in every situation, by prayer and petition, with thanksgiving, present your requests to God. (Philippians 4:6)*

Remember Bartimaeus the blind man who sat by the side of the road. The Bible tells us that many rebuked him, telling him to be quiet, but instead of heading their voice, he shouted even more, "Son of David, have mercy on me!" The result of his courageous persistence led to the restoration of his sight (Mark 10:46-52).

Another example of faithful persistence is found in Mark Chapter 2. Jesus was preaching in Capernaum when a large crowd gathered to hear Him. The crowd was so large that no one else could enter the house He was in. And so, four men carried their paralyzed friend through the crowd, dug a hole in the roof, and lowered Him down to Jesus so that he might be healed.

The anointed move forward regardless of what it might cost. We've seen this in every chapter of this study. In fact, we see it in the life of every faithful believer who takes up their cross.

THE KEY TO PERSISTENCE

The best things rarely come easy. They take up our time, they call us to sacrifice, and they are inconvenient at times. But as we see in the scriptures, lives were changed because they chose God.

How many times do we give up when we should have pressed on? How many opportunities have we missed out on because we didn't have the courage to take the next step? The key to persistence is faith. Faith in the power of God to fix what we can't.

JACOB AND ESAU

In Genesis 27, we find the story of Jacob and Esau. After trading a bowl of stew for his brother's birthright, Jacob deceived his father to gain his blessing. Isaac was old by this time, and his eyesight had failed. And so, with the help of his mother, Rebecca, Jacob clothed himself in goatskin to mimic Esau's hairy appearance. He went to Isaac with food and wine, and after he kissed his father, Jacob received a blessing that Isaac couldn't reverse.

When Esau heard his father's words, he burst out with a loud and bitter cry and said to his father, "Bless me—me too, my father!" But he said, "Your brother came deceitfully and took your blessing." (Genesis 27:34-35)

Esau was angry that day. So angry in fact, that the Bible tells us he intended to kill Jacob. "The days of mourning for my father are near; then I will kill my brother Jacob," he said.

Because of that threat, Jacob left home to live with his uncle Laban. It was there he met his two wives, Rachel, and Leah, and started a family with them.

DID YOU KNOW

ACCORDING TO DEUTERONOMY 21:17, THE OLDEST CHILD WAS ENTITLED TO A DOUBLE SHARE IN HIS FATHER'S INHERITANCE. AND SO, WHEN ESAU SOLD HIS BIRTHRIGHT, HE SOLD BOTH THE RIGHT TO HIS INCREASED INHERITANCE AND A SPECIAL BLESSING FROM ISAAC.

Years later, Jacob got word that his brother Esau was coming to see him, and of course, he was rightly concerned. Horrified perhaps when he heard that Esau was coming with 400 men.

This story happened thousands of years ago—I know that—but I also know this,

> *Everything that was written in the past was written to teach us, so that through the endurance taught in the scriptures and the encouragement they provide we might have hope. (Romans 15:4)*

The scriptures say that faith comes by hearing and hearing by the word of God, because we are strengthened by the faith of those like Jacob who have humbled themselves before God.

Maybe you don't have an army of 400 men marching toward you, and hopefully you haven't experienced family drama to this extent, but chances are you've had friction in a relationship at some point in your life. Whether it was a broken marriage, a fragmented family, problems in your workplace, or a friendship that ended in pain, you know the heartache it causes, and the courage it takes to reconcile that which is lost.

IN THE PALM OF GOD'S HAND

No one can soften a stone-cold heart or subdue a mighty army the way that God can. We can love them, and we can pray for them, but that's where it ends for us. The rest is in the palm of God's hand to do with as He will.

> *In the LORD's hand the king's heart is a stream of water that he channels toward all who please him. (Proverbs 21:1)*

There's no mistaking the fact that Esau's heart was softened that day. There is no doubt that God went before Jacob to pave the way for reconciliation. The Bible tells us that Esau ran to meet Jacob, embraced him, and kissed him on the neck.

I WILL GO BEFORE YOU
AND WILL LEVEL THE MOUNTAINS;
I WILL BREAK DOWN GATES OF BRONZE
AND CUT THROUGH BARS OF IRON.
(ISAIAH 45:2)

JACOB REFUSED TO GIVE UP

For some, the story ends there, but before we move on, let's turn back a chapter to Genesis 32, which takes place the night before he meets Esau. Notice Jacob's persistence. The Bible tells us that that he wrestled with God until daybreak. While they wrestled, Jacob dislocated his hip, but still he wouldn't let go. He knew how important it was to persist, and so he refused to give up on God, until he was blessed.

Some days it seems like our problems are long past the point of repair. Other days it feels like the journey ahead is out of our hands. And it is, which is why we all need to persistently pray and trust in Him Who is paving the way. The One Who knows what tomorrow will bring. The One Who wrote it all down before we were born.

Bring it to God today, bring it to Him tomorrow, bring it to Him the next day and the day beyond that. Don't give up on God. Take your burden to Him and lay it down at His feet.

God told Jacob to return to his homeland, and so he was doing just that. Yes—he was scared, but unlike others who might have given up and turned back, He faithfully turned to the Lord. He struggled with God, and he didn't quit until he was blessed.

The more I study this chapter, the more I'm impressed by Jacob's actions. Verse after verse, he lays out a pattern for overcoming one's fear. And so, it's important to pause for a minute, to consider the things he did well.

As you pause and reflect on the next few pages, take a personal approach to answering the questions. We're looking at five steps that Jacob took to overcome fear. As we look at each one, ask yourself what you can learn from his example as well as any practical ways you might apply it to your life.

For it is the LORD your God who goes with you; He will never leave you nor forsake you.

Deut. 31:6

Step 1: Jacob was afraid, but even so, he was willing to follow God's command to return home.

In great fear and distress Jacob divided the people who were with him into two groups, and the flocks and herds and camels as well. (Genesis 32:7)

What can you learn from Jacob's example here?

What does Philippians 2:8 say?

Step 2: When Jacob was afraid, he turned to prayer, both expressing his feelings to the Lord, and asking God to help him.

Save me, I pray, from the hand of my brother Esau, for I am afraid he will come and attack me, and also the mothers with their children. (Genesis 32:11)

What can you learn from Jacob's example here?

What does Psalm 46:1 say?

Step 3: He trusted in the promise from God and leaned into that promise when he needed strength.

But you have said, 'I will surely make you prosper and will make your descendants like the sand of the sea, which cannot be counted.' (Genesis 32:12)

What can you learn from Jacob's example here?

What does Hebrews 10:23 say?

Step 4: He wrestled with God until he was blessed.

Then the man said, "Let me go, for it is daybreak." But Jacob replied, "I will not let you go unless you bless me." (Genesis 32:26)

What can you learn from Jacob's example here?

What does Luke 18:7 say?

Step 5: Before asking God for a blessing, Jacob made a conscious effort to reconcile with Esau by sending a gift to him.

He spent the night there, and from what he had with him he selected a gift for his brother Esau: two hundred female goats and twenty male goats, two hundred ewes and twenty rams, thirty female camels with their young, forty cows and ten bulls, and twenty female donkeys and ten male donkeys. (Genesis 32:13)

What can we learn from Jacob's example here?

What does Matthew 5:23-24 say?

Put on the full armor of God, so that when the day of evil comes, you may be able to stand your ground, and after you have done everything, to stand.

Ephesians 6:13

Chapter Nine

PREPARING FOR BATTLE

Read: 2 Chronicles 29-32

What do you know about Hezekiah? After reading this chapter, you'll know he was righteous, you'll see that he was courageous, and you'll understand why he's been hailed as one of Judah's greatest kings. You'll see that he made every effort to put God first and to serve the needs of his kingdom by bringing their burdens to God. He wasn't perfect, but he was repentant and because of that, he was blessed.

To understand the story of Hezekiah, and the reason he stands out as one of the most courageous men in the Bible, we need to look at who the Assyrians were and what they were capable of. We've read all kinds of stories in the Bible about the battles between Israel and the enemies that came up against them, but none were as terrifying as the Assyrian army.

Known as "The Lords of Torture," Historians describe their methods of war as vicious, sadistic, and cruel. Adults and young children alike were captured, impaled, skinned, beheaded, castrated, and burned alive. Images depict Assyrian soldiers forcing Babylonian captives to grind the bones of their families. Others show prisoners being led by chains attached to hooks in their mouths. And, as we see in 2 Chronicles Chapter 32, they used psychological warfare to threaten and discourage those who might come up against them.

2 Kings 18:5 says,

There was no one like him among all the kings of Judah,
either before him or after him.

THE COURAGE TO CHANGE

His first order of business as King was to open the doors of the temple and cleanse it. This wasn't the easiest thing for Hezekiah to do since the temple had been closed for several years. The Israelites had forsaken their faith and turned their back on the Lord. And so, in a sense, he was introducing a new way of life for the people of Israel.

Many of them had grown accustomed to the ways of King Ahaz who shut the doors of the temple, set up altars at every street corner in Jerusalem, and burned sacrifices to other gods. Idol worship was their way of life, and now they were being shown something different.

In 2 Chronicles 30, Hezekiah sent invitations to the people of Israel inviting them to return to the Lord, and while many of them did, others scorned and ridiculed his messengers.

Hezekiah is an example to all new believers who face opposition when they begin their journey through faith. Turning our back on the sinful life we once knew, takes courage. Friends may distance themselves; others might ridicule and scoff the new faith that we've found.

It can be hard when friends and family desert us, which is why we need people like Hezekiah to encourage us in our faith. He did what was right in the sight of the Lord regardless of the opposition he faced. And what did they experience as they worshipped the Lord? Incredible joy, unlike anything they had seen in years!

> *There was great joy in Jerusalem, for since the days of Solomon, son of David king of Israel there had been nothing like this in Jerusalem. (2 Chronicles 30:26)*

WHEN HEZEKIAH CAME TO THE CROWN, HE APPLIED AT ONCE TO WORK REFORM. THOSE WHO BEGIN WITH GOD, BEGIN AT THE RIGHT END OF THEIR WORK, AND IT WILL PROSPER ACCORDINGLY.

—MATTHEW HENRY

FASHIONED LIKE CLAY

With faithfulness comes tribulation, for it's through temptation we learn faithfulness; through poverty we find contentment; and in fear we find our courage. If we hope to be strong, we must first be reliant. And so, before Hezekiah could be a great king, he had to humble himself before God. Molded and made, he was fashioned like clay in the hands of a potter.

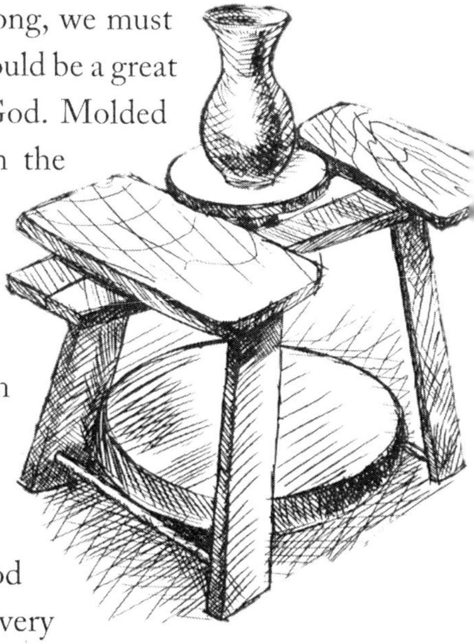

Charles Spurgeon once said,

> "Whenever God means to make a man great, He always breaks him in pieces first. I want to comfort you by showing you that this is God's way of making something of you... That spade will cut sharply and dig up sod after sod and throw it to one side. The very thing you would like to keep shall be cast away and you shall be hollowed out, and dug out, that the word of Elisha may be fulfilled, 'Make this valley full of ditches. For thus says the Lord, you shall not see wind, neither shall you see rain; yet that valley shall be filled with water.' You are to be tried, my Friend, that God may be glorified in you!"

And so, Hezekiah was met with opposition. The resistance from the people of Israel, however, was nothing compared to the trial he faced when he took a stand against the king of Assyria.

DO NOT BE AFRAID

To encourage someone is to instill courage in them, which is what Hezekiah did before taking a stand against the Assyrians. The Bible tells us that he appointed miliary officers over the people and encouraged them with these words,

Do not be afraid or discouraged because of the king of Assyria and the vast army with him, for there is a greater power with us than with him. (2 Chronicles 32:6)

These are practically the same words that John used in his letter as he encouraged the church,

You, dear children, are from God and have overcome them, because the one who is in you is greater than the one who is in the world. (1 John 4:4)

NO WEAPON FORGED AGAINST YOU WILL PREVAIL, AND YOU WILL REFUTE EVERY TONGUE THAT ACCUSES YOU. THIS IS THE HERITAGE OF THE SERVANTS OF THE LORD. (ISAIAH 54:17)

Hezekiah continues,

With him is only the arm of flesh, but with us is the Lord our God to help us and to fight our battles." And the people gained confidence from what Hezekiah the king of Judah said. (2 Chronicles 32:8)

Hezekiah reminded them that they weren't fighting alone. He knew that the power of God was greater than any power on earth, and that God would protect and sustain them.

Regardless of what you are up against, and whatever it is you might fear, whether it's a person coming for you or a problem that you doubt you can solve, you can always be sure that your problems are no match for God.

PREPARE FOR THE BATTLE

Hezekiah prepared for the battle. 2 Chronicles 32, tells us that he gathered a group of people and together they blocked off the water that flowed through the land. They prepared the broken sections of the wall and built towers on it. They reinforced the wall around the city and built a second wall around that. They made many weapons and shields.

DID YOU KNOW

PART OF A WALL WHICH COULD WELL BE HEZEKIAH'S HAS BEEN UNCOVERED ON THE WESTERN HILL. AT SEVEN METRES THICK, IT IS THE THICKEST IRON AGE WALL KNOWN IN PALESTINE. (MARK SELMAN'S COMMENTARY ON 2 CHRONICLES)

Adversity does one of two things: it either strengthens us or it defeats us, and if you're not strong in your faith, you won't be strong in the fight. And so, we need to prepare for tomorrow's battle today. Holding on to the joy that flows like a river from the Spirit within. Reinforcing the walls of protection by drawing closer to God. Standing firm in our faith with every weapon and shield that we have.

> *Therefore, put on the full armor of God, so that when the day of evil comes, you may be able to stand your ground, and after you have done everything, to stand. (Ephesians 6:13)*

DID YOU KNOW

GOD DESTROYED THE ASSYRIAN ARMY WITHOUT HEZEKIAH AND HIS MEN LIFTING A HAND. 2 KINGS 19:35 TELLS US THAT THE ANGEL OF THE LORD SMOTE 185,000 OF THEIR MEN IN ONE NIGHT.

IT WAS NOT BY THEIR SWORD THAT THEY WON THE LAND, NOR DID THEIR ARM BRING THEM VICTORY; IT WAS YOUR RIGHT HAND, YOUR ARM, AND THE LIGHT OF YOUR FACE, FOR YOU LOVED THEM. (PSALM 44:3)

PAUSE AND REFLECT

What was his first order of business as king?

How was King Hezekiah different from his father?

What happened to the messengers in 2 Chronicles Chapter 30 when they delivered the invitations on behalf of King Hezekiah?

What does 1 Peter 4:14 say? Write the verse out here:

What steps did Hezekiah take to prepare for the battle?

What does 1 Peter 4:14 say? Write the verse out here:

How should we prepare for tomorrow's battle today?

What does the word encourage mean?

What does the word discourage mean?

According to Romans 15:4, what 2 things give us hope?

What are the six (let's make that seven) pieces of armor listed in Ephesians 6:10-18?

1.

2.

3.

4.

5.

6.

7.

What happened after Hezekiah and Isaiah prayed?

But he said to me,
"My grace is sufficient
for you, for my power is
made perfect inweakness."
Therefore I will
boast all the more
gladly about my
weaknesses, so that
Christ's power may
rest on me.
2 Corinthins 12:9

Chapter Ten

GETTING PAST THE "BUT"

Read: Nehemiah 1-3

We've all had a feeling of uncertainty at times. Wondering what we'll do next. Wondering where God will lead. Wondering how things could possibly change when all we've been given are the two hands that we've got. Longing to succeed, yet not having the courage or the power to do so.

Opening our Bibles to Nehemiah, we find a man with nothing but passion and prayer. A man whose desire for change ran so deep that he wept and mourned and fasted for days.

The Bible tells us that he was a cupbearer to the King. He wasn't a king himself; he wasn't the captain of a large army, he didn't have the necessary resources at his disposal to rebuild the walls of Jerusalem, but he had faith in a God Who makes the impossible possible.

That kind of faith unlocks the door to our courage. It reminds us that the power within us is far greater than anything that could potentially stand in our way.

HE WAS AFRAID, BUT...

Notice the words that Nehemiah uses in Chapter 2:

"I was very much afraid, but..."

He wasn't just afraid—he was very terrified. Nehemiah knew that his attitude in the king's presence was a serious matter, and that disappointing the king could result in negative consequences.

DID YOU KNOW

A PERSIAN SUBJECT WAS EXPECTED TO BE PERFECTLY CONTENT SO LONG AS HE HAD THE HAPPINESS OF BEING WITH HIS KING. A REQUEST TO QUIT THE COURT WAS THUS A SERIOUS MATTER.

—BARNES NOTES ON THE BIBLE

When the king asked Nehemiah why he looked unhappy, a window of opportunity opened for him to either plead his case, or step back and let someone else fulfill his mission.

Once again, I'm reminded of the verse from the story of Esther that we discussed in Chapter 3,

For if you remain silent at this time, relief and deliverance for the Jews will arise from another place, but you and your father's family

will perish. And who knows but that you have come to your royal position for such a time as this? (Esther 4:14)

Like Esther, Nehemiah was in the king's palace, and like her he had an opportunity to use his position to glorify God.

"But" is a powerful word, and depending on how we use it, we can either step forward in faith, or step back in fear. Nehemiah was terrified, but despite his fear he spoke to the king.

Like Nehemiah, we need to start using that word when it comes to the things we fear most:

I'm afraid, but I'll follow God's will.
I'm standing alone, but I'll keep standing strong.
I can't do this, but God can.
They might ridicule me, but I'm choosing to follow the Lord.
I don't know where my next paycheck will come from, but I am trusting that God will provide.
I'm afraid to speak to my boss, but I know God is with me.
I'm worried about my kids, but I'll leave them in God's capable hands.
My problem is big, but my God is bigger.
I've lost someone dear, but I'll see them again.

DID YOU KNOW

MANY SCHOLARS BELIEVE THAT NEHEMIAH WAS IN THE PALACE AT SUSA AT THE SAME TIME IN HISTORY AS ESTHER, WHICH MEANS THAT THEIR PATHS MAY HAVE CROSSED.

We need to remind ourselves, and then keep reminding ourselves that we are not in control. Nehemiah wasn't *lucky* that the king was favorable to his request, he was graciously blessed by God Who was working to pave the way.

> *And because the gracious hand of my God was on me, the king granted my requests. (Nehemiah 2:8b)*

A PARALLEL TO OUR FAITH

As we get into Chapter 3 of Nehemiah, we see that they've started building the walls. What's interesting to note here is that the book of Nehemiah is a parallel of sorts to the work of the Holy Spirit in purifying our heart, renewing our mind, and leading us through spiritual warfare. In the same way that the walls of Jerusalem protected the temple from the enemy, self-control is a way of protecting our hearts and our minds from the enemy. When we come to Christ, we start rebuilding those walls. We examine our hearts in the same way that Nehemiah examined the walls in Chapter 2, and we strengthen them in the same way that Hezekiah did in the previous chapter.

The Bible draws a comparison between self-control (governing our passions) and the walls of a city when it says,

> *He that hath no rule over his own spirit is like a city that is broken down, and without walls. (Proverbs 25:28)*

In MacLaren's Expositions we read,

> "He who submits himself to Christ is lord of himself as none else are. He has a light within which teaches him what is sin. He has a love within which puts out the flame of temptation, as the sun does a coal fire. He has a motive to resist; he has power for resistance; he has hope in resisting. Only thus are the walls broken down rebuilded."

In Nehemiah 4:2, we see the enemy trying everything he can to stop their work. Hurling insults as he questions their ability.

> *What are those feeble Jews doing? Will they restore their wall? Will they offer sacrifices? Will they finish in a day? Can they bring the stones back to life from those heaps of rubble—burned as they are?*

SATAN IS USING THE SAME TACTICS

When we submit ourselves to Christ, and as we're building that wall around the temple to protect us from the enemy, we're going to face opposition. We've all been there. We've heard the things that people say about Christians. And, whether they say it to our face or not, we know that the enemy is out there trying to discourage us from completing the work God has called us to.

To discourage someone is to take their courage away. That's exactly what the enemy is trying to do when we are mocked, insulted, and attacked. And, while the discouragement often comes from those outside our faith, some days that voice can be heard from within.

> *I can't do it.*
> *I'm afraid.*
> *I'm not good enough.*
> *I don't measure up.*
> *I'm going to fail.*
> *I'm too old.*
> *I don't have the resources.*
> *This is too hard for someone like me.*

Compare these discouraging thoughts to the attack from the enemies in Nehemiah Chapter 4, and you will see that Satan is using the same tactics of intimidation today that he used back then.

Notice the first thing that Nehemiah does when he is faced with opposition—he prays, and he posts a guard. This is exactly what Jesus told His disciples to do on the night He was betrayed.

> *Watch and pray so that you will not fall into temptation. The spirit is willing, but the flesh is weak. (Mark 14:38)*

Jesus knew that they would be standing against the enemy that very night, and He also knew that prayer was the best source of protection for them.

Whether we realize it or not, there's a war taking place in the spiritual realm. While God is at work in our lives, there's an enemy with a bow in his hand, and he's aiming straight for our hearts. And so, our first thought should always be prayer. Whether we're folding laundry, standing at the kitchen sink washing dishes, or driving in our cars, we must be armed and ready for battle.

Likewise, in Ephesians 6, after Paul encourages the church to put on the full armor of God, he reminds them to watch and pray,

> *Praying always with all prayer and supplication in the Spirit, and watching thereunto with all perseverance and supplication for all saints. (Ephesians 6:18)*

There are going to be days when the enemy is attacking us from all sides. Situations that try our patience and test our will. Days when we're afraid to step out in faith. Times when we question our worth and doubt our ability.

On days like that remember Nehemiah, who courageously spoke to the king despite his fear. Remember how he ignored the enemies that desperately tried to discourage him. Finally, following Nehemiah's example, take your eyes off the world, and take your burdens to prayer.

THE DEVIL WILL TRY YOU, BUT HE WON'T BE TRIUMPHANT. NOT AS LONG AS YOU'RE STANDING WITH GOD AND STANDING IN FAITH.

—DARLENE SCHACHT

PAUSE AND REFLECT

What are some of the "buts" that have held you back the past?

What did Nehemiah do first when he heard that his people were in trouble, and their city broken down?

What two things did Nehemiah do when he was faced with opposition?

What does Matthew 6:34 say? Write the verse out here:

What advice does James 4:7 give us regarding the enemy?

Looking back on this study, what are some important things you learned about courage?

Made in United States
North Haven, CT
19 June 2023

37954427R00080